SIGURÐR:
REBIRTH AND THE
RITES OF TRANSFORMATION

SIGURÐR:
REBIRTH AND THE
RITES OF TRANSFORMATION

by

STEPHEN E. FLOWERS

Based on a Thesis Presented to the Faculty of the Graduate School of
The University of Texas at Austin in Partial Fulfillment of the
Requirements for the Degree of
MASTER OF ARTS
THE UNIVERSITY OF TEXAS AT AUSTIN
May 1979

Published by
LODESTAR
P.O. Box 16
Bastrop, Texas 78602

www.seekthemystery.com

PREFACE TO THE 2011 EDITION

The Master's Thesis upon which this text is based was originally entitled "Rebirth and Rites of Transformation in the Saga of Sigurðr Sigmundarson." It was supervised by the renowned scholars John M. Weinstock and Edgar Polomé at the University of Texas at Austin in 1979. The work was produced within the Department of Germanic Languages and Literature. It is as much a work belonging to the study of the history of religion and myth as it is a work of Germanic philology.

The major value of this work is twofold: First is is one of the most comprehensive treatments of the concept of the soul in northern Germanic tradition ever produced in English and second, it demonstrates the functionality of these concepts in the context of the process of rebirth, as conceived of by the early medieval peoples of Scandinavia.

More than thirty years have past since the thesis upon which this text is based was written. Over the years this obscure text has had some interesting influences. Among them is the notation that a popular writer, Stephan Grundy, in his novel *Rhinegold*, acknowledged the influence of the work on the substance of his book.

The manuscript version of this work was released in the 1980s for a limited time, but since then it has remained a hidden text. I noted with some pleasure when I recently visited the library stacks where this text is stored at the University of Texas, that the pages were tattered and that it had been checked out dozens of times over the years since it was completed.

I have left most of the text as it was with no bibliographical or substantial improvements, only smoothing it out for readability here and there. I trust that this work will continue to find readers who will make use of its contents.

Stephen E. Flowers
Woodharrow
January 13, 2011

Abbreviations

AaNo	*Aarboger for Nordisk Oldkyndighed og Historie*
AG	*Acta Germanica*
Akv.	"Atlakviða"
ANF	*Arkiv för Nordisk Filologi*
Bdr.	"Baldrs daumar"
BGDSL	*Beiträge zur Geschichte der deutschen Sprache und Literatur*
ch./chs.	chapter/chapters
CR	*Codex Regius*
ESS	*Edda Snorra Sturlusonar*
FAS	*Fornaldarsögur*
Flb.	*Flateyjarbók*
Fm.	"Fáfnismál"
Frühmast.	*Frühmittelalterliche Studien*
GA	*Germanische Abhandlungen*
Gmc.	Germanic
Go.	Gothic
GRM	*Germanish-romanische Monatsschrift*
Grp.	"Grípisspá"
Háv.	"Hávamál"
HHI	"Helgakviða Hundingsbana I"
HHII	"Helgakviða Hundingsbana II"
HHj.	"Helgakviða Hjörvarðssonar"
Hkr.	*Heimskringla*
Hrólfs s. kr.	*Hrólfs saga krraka*
IE	Indo-European
ÍS	*Íslendingasögur*
JEGP	*Journal of English and Germanic Philology*
KS	*Konungasögur*
MLN	*Modern Language Notes*
MM	*Maal og Minne*
MScan.	*Medieval Scandinavia*
NE	New English
NL	*Nibelungenlied*
Nph.	*Neophilologus*
Nþ.	*Nornagestsþáttr*
OE	Old English
OFris.	Old Frisian

OHG	Old High German
OIr.	Old Irish
ON	Old Norse
OS	Old Saxon
RGA	*Reallexikon der germanischen Altertumskunde*
Rm.	"Reginsmál"
Rs.	"Regin smiður"
Rþ.	"Rígsþula'
Sd.	"Sigrdrífumál"
Sg.	"Sigurðarkviða in skamma"
st./sts.	stanza/stanzas
SS	*Scandinavian Studies*
ÞS	*Þiðrekssaga*
Vkv.	"Völundarkviða"
Vm.	"Vafðuðnismál"
Vsp.	"Völuspá"
Yngl. s.	*Ynglings saga*
ZDA	*Zeitschrift für deutsches Altertum*
ZDP	*Zeitschrift für deutsche Philologie*

CHAPTER ONE

INTRODUCTION

Sigurðr Fáfnisbáni is perhaps the greatest heroic figure produced by the Germanic world of myth. His father Sigmundr Völsungarson himself foretold that his son would be "the foremost of our [the Völsungs] clan," and that his "name will live as long as the world endures."(1) This prophecy has proven to be true, for no figure has been more consistently portrayed and revived throughout so many centuries of Germanic literary and ideological history, as has been the figure of Sigurðr the Dragon-Slayer.(2) A question remains as to why the Sigurðr myth was considered to be such an exemplary model, and it is hoped that this work will provide a satisfactory reply to at least a portion of this question.

The present work endeavors to demonstrate that Sigurðr is in fact the rebirth,(3) (*aftrburðr*) of his father, Sigmundr. Toward this end it is necessary to examine the Norse conceptions of the human "soul(s)" as they are important to the understanding of the ideology of "rebirth." Furthermore, this work intends to outline the initial phase of Sigurðr's heroic career (from his birth through the *Vaterrache* episode), and proceed to interpret the various events in this phase as a series of rites of transformation.(4) It seems that these initial rites of transformation serve, in part, to (re-)integrate Sigurðr into his ancestral divine paradigm/archetype, and then lead him to become fully "conscious" of, or perhaps more correctly, to fully manifest the previous paradigmatic transformations and powers present in his father. The implications of these mythic models for archaic Germanic society also play an important role in the discussions and final interpretations.

It would perhaps serve some good purpose to state at the outset what this work is not intended to demonstrate. It is not intended to serve as an analysis of the archaic conceptions of the Germanic soul *in toto*, but only certain portions of it. There is also no attempt to reconstruct an "original" literary(5) or mythic(6) archetype for the saga of Sigurd/Siegfried. Nor are all the aspects of the rites of transformation discussed, but only those dealing directly with *aftrburðr*. The relatively coherent and mythically authentic version given in the *VS-CR* will be closely followed, in order to keep hypothetical speculation concerning form to a minimum. Moreover, it is not intended to make any final conclusions concerning an comprehensive interpretation of the *Sigurðarsaga*(7) or to discuss the full implications of the aspects of cosmological symbolism(8) as it relates to the religious-historical symbolism, which is more central to this work. In many cases various technical terms may best be defined within the contexts of the chapters in which they are introduced. There are, however, some special terms which may be found throughout the text, and which should be provisionally clarified from the outset. These definitions are not intended to be universal, nor even complete within the context of this work, but rather they should provide a degree of general clarification of the way in which these terms are used in this work:

1) Archetype/paradigm. Both of these terms are used to indicate exemplary models of one kind or another. In the case of the term "archetype" these models are the "primordial images" as defined by C. G. Jung and E. Neumann,(9) and they are usually perceived as animate entities. "Paradigm" on the other hand is used more often in inanimate, structural contexts. However, in certain contexts, when the meaning is clear, either term may be used.

2) Function. This important term may be understood in one of three ways: a) in a non-specialized sense, as the characteristic action of something or someone; b) in the Dumézilian sense, with reference to the archaic, tripartite Indo-European ideological principle of socio-theological classification;(10) c) Chapter V introduces a classificatory system for the various functions of the souls) within the psychosomatic complex. The purpose of this system is akin to that of the Dumézilian system, i.e., to distinguish characteristic action from name in order to obtain a clearer picture of the archetype or paradigm in question.(11)

3) Initiation. This term basically denotes the transition from one ontological state of being to another, in conformity with a divine archetype or cosmological paradigm. The initiate is admitted into various levels or institutions within a society, a body of magico-religious knowledge, or a type of divine power. The types and purposes of such initiations are extremely varied, but a constant characteristic is the aspect of change or metamorphosis—the initiate is profoundly and permanently changed as he/she makes a transition from one ontological state of being to another. Symbolic representations of death and rebirth are often present in these paradigms, however, this is not obligatory.(12) The presence of

'masters' and/or divine beings, which aid in the process, is also almost universal.

4) Rites of Transformation (Rites of Passage). This formula, as outlined by Arnold van Gennep(13) is similar to the definition of "initiation" given above, if somewhat more structuralized. Van Gennep's ideas concerning the process of separation, transition (initiation proper), and incorporation play an important role in this work. Here, the formulaic expression "rites of transformation" itself refers to a process or series of initiations. Such a process may belong to any one of several levels in society. There are the common rites of passage (birth–puberty–marriage–death [funeral]). Furthermore, there might also be found heroic (martial) and "shamanistic,"(14) (mystical) rites of transformation peculiar to certain secret societies within a given culture. These rites often have numerous correspondences with the common rites of passage, both with regard to the general sequence of rites and to their internal structures. It must be pointed out that this work does not postulate that this section of the story of Sigurðr represents a continuous ritual text, or that it ever did, but rather that the written documents which we have are at best samples of the mythic lore imparted during initiations,(15) and which might portray the exemplary model for the initiate and the initiatory process in a narrative form. At worst these documents are the reflections of what later generations perceived the archaic beliefs to have been.(16) In either case the texts do not seem to represent a continuous ritual process, but rather a series of processes are portrayed, which outline or illustrate initiatory themes, rituals or sacro-legal actions common in the Germanic world.

5) Mythological authenticity. This term indicates that a motif is genuine within its own theological and/or cosmological context, and that if it is not an entirely indigenous concept, it is in any event firmly established and syncretized in conformity with the paradigmatic and archetypal laws of the cosmos in which it is found.

6) Cultural authority. This is analogous to the definition of mythological authenticity presented above, except that here we are dealing with cultural and ethnological contexts rather than cosmological and theological ones. This also implies that a motif has found general acceptance within a given culture.

The interpretations suggested in Chapter VIII are often presented under three classificatory headings, for each of which clarification seems in order:

1) The socio-cultic aspects are concerned with the representation of formal cultic practices and social aspects of the internal cultic structure and the relationship of that cult to the larger society in which it functions.

2) The mythological aspects relate to "the world of the gods" and the cosmos, that is, archaic (Germanic) theology, its archetypes, paradigms, laws, and ethics, and archaic (Germanic) cosmology with its basic concepts. 3) The psycho-magical aspects are concerned with the realm of the human "psyche" or the archetypal "psyche," and the processes which it undergoes in order to transmute itself from one state of being to another. This refers more to the internal psychic processes which affect the initiate—both human and archetypal. Of course, in the case of the archetype the process and the "initiate" could be understood as being assimilated to one another.

The general methods of interpretation and modes of observation used in formulating this work are those outlined by Mircia Eliade(17) and Joseph Campbell.(18) Arnold van Gennep's seminal text, *The Rites of Passage*, also exercises its fundamental influence on the present work. As regards Germanic mythology, the interpretations and observations of Jan de Vries(19) and Vilhelm Grönbech(20) have proven to be most influential.

Indeed it seems that Sigurðr is the *aftrburðr* of Sigmundr, and that this phase of the saga describes a paradigmatic transformational process by which Sigurðr is integrated into his ancestral archetype and into the *hamingja* and/or *fylgja*(21) of his clan. Several of the texts dealt with here, especially the *Codex Regius* (and other Eddic material), and the *Völsungasaga*, are often best approached not as "literature," but rather as cultural documents, or intellectual artifacts.(22) The texts portraying this phase of the story of Sigurðr appear to describe two continuous paradigmatic processes, a mythological drama and a psycho-magical development, and both of these are supported by a series of socio-cultic rites.(23) However, it must be emphasized that for the archaic Germanic world, all of these processes were essentially understood within a sacred(24) context.

Footnotes to Chapter One

1. *VS.* ch. 12:137-38. *"fremstr af várri ætt ... (hans) nafn mun uppi, meðan veröldin stendr."*

2. Besides the six major texts recorded in Nordic dialects discussed below, there also exist numerous other texts concerned with the saga of Sigurðr. In Norway and Sweden there exist ballads called "Sigurd Svein" which were recorded in the 16th-century, but which date from around 1300, while in Denmark ballads called "Sivard Snarensvend" and "Sivard og Brynhild" (for which Norwegian fragments exist) appear at approximately the same time. Also in Denmark there is a Danish translation of a lost Latin text, known as the *Hven Chronicle* (ca. 1603). However, this is mainly concerned with the later *Niflungasaga*. The figure of Sigurðr is also well attested in the southern Germanic region. Works from this southern branch present a divergent tradition, and one which evolved over several centuries: *Das Nibelungenlied* (ca. 1200), "Siefrid de Ardemont" by Albrecht von Scharfenberg (ca. 1280), this work is found in Ulrich Fuetrer's *Buch der Abenteuer*, which contains a late 15th-century reduction, *Das Lied vom hurnen Seyfrid* (ca. 1520), *Der Hurnen Seufrid* by Hans Sachs (1557) and the *Volksbuch vom gehörnten Sigfrid* (printed 1726). The figure of Sigurðr is also prevalent in more modern literature. In Germany Sigurðr is represented in Friedrich Hebbel's drama *Die Nibelungen* (1861), in Richard Wagner's drama *Siegfrieds Tod* and of course in his operatic tetrology *Der Ring des Nibelungen* (first performed 1876), and most recently in Max Mell's drama *Der Nibelunge Not* (1943, 1951). Henrik Ibsen also helped fulfill Sigmundr's prophecy when he portrayed Sigurd in *Hærmædene på Helgeland*, and some see the spirit of Sigurðr in many of Ibsen's later dramas as well. In England Sigurðr was reborn in 1877 in William Morris' poem *Sigurd*. This body of literature coupled with the evidence of plastic representations of the story of Sigurðr found in Norway (carvings from the churches of Ostad, Veigusdal, Lardal, and Hyllestad), in Sweden (the inscriptions on the stones of Dräule, Ramsjö, and Ockelbo, and the door of Värsås church), in England (the Halton Cross near Lancaster) and on the Isle of Man (the Andreas Cross), and many others, all demonstrate the wide distribution of, and the deep affection for, the figure of Sigurðr Fáfnisbani. (Cf. Schück (193-) I, 171 for illustrations of these artifacts.) Sigurðr must indeed be regarded as *the* Germanic hero *par excellence*, that is at least in the northern tradition.

3. For a definition of ´rebirth´ see Chapter V.

4. For a definition of "rites of transformation" see below in this chapter.

5. For a discussion of the literary archetype of the Nibelungen material, see Mary Thorp "The Archetype of the Nibelungen legend." *JEGP* 37 (1938), 7-17.

6. The problem of mythic archetypes and mythological themes in the Nibelungen material is discussed by K. Lachmann (1829),446 ff., K. Müllenhoff (1879),146 ff., F. R. Schröder (1919), 1 ff., F. R. Schröder (1955), 1 ff., K. Steiger (1873), 33, F. Panzer (1955), 285 ff., and H. M. and N. K. Chadwick (1940), 138, while a more general study of mythic archetypes in "history" may be found M. Eliade (1971), 34 ff. *et passim*.

7. For general interpretations, cf. the works mentioned above for mythological or folkloristic interpretations; cf. also O. Höfler (1961), 13 ff., for a mytho-historical interpretation. There also exists a body of literature which interprets the story of Sigurðr in light of historical events of the *Völkerwanderungszeit*. Interpretations of this type are to be found in L. Ernst (1839), H. Kuhn (1953), and G. Schütle (1921), 291 ff., all of which identify Sigurðr-Sigfrid with Sigibert of Austrasia (†575). Sigurðr = Araja the Ostrogoth for R. Huss (1923), 506 ff., and M. Lintzel (1935). G. Vigfusson and G. Y. Powell (1886), and A. Beneke *Siegfried ist Armin!* (1911), along with O. Höfler (1961) in a special sense, identify Sigurðr as Arminius, while A. Crüger (1841) believes that Victorinus served as the model for Sigurðr. H. de Boor (1972), xxiv ff., and (1939), 250 ff., tries to demon-strate that the Burgundian material is an integral part of the saga and not a later addition.

8. Cosmological symbolism plays an important role in the interpretation of K. Steiger (1873) as well as in the interpretations of many who follow him.

9. E. Neumann (1954), xv, defines the archetypes as "the structural elements of the collective unconscious. ... They are the pictorial forms of the instincts, for the unconscious reveals itself to the conscious mind in images." For a more exhaustive definition see C. G. Jung (1959), 3 ff., *et passim*.

10. The Dumézilian concept "function" is discussed in general by C. S. Littleton (1973), 4-6. "The term "function," as Dumézil uses it, refers in the last analysis to neither the social strata, the behavior of their occupants, nor their divine representations. Rather, it refers to the principles in terms of which these phenomena are defined." (p. 5).

11. This classificatory system is not necessarily Dumézilian with regard to structure or content.

12. For a general discussion of initiation see M. Eliade (1958), ix-xv, 1-4, *et passim*.

13. A. van Gennep (1960 [1909]), 1-13, *et passim*. A more modern discussion, with direct reference to Gmc. material is forwarded by L. Gruber (1977), 330-340.

14. Here "shamanism" is used in its most general meaning, cf. M. Eliade (1972), 87-89.

15. See M. Eliade (1958), x-xv, *et passim*, for a general discussion of the role of lore in the initiatory process.

16. The *VS*, and of course the *CR* both preserve an abundance of archaic, pre-Christian symbolism, structure, and content, however, the hand of a later (most probably at least nominally Christian) editor is evident in the MSS. of both works.

17. See the bibliography for a list of works by M. Eliade consulted for this work.

18. Joseph Campbell's study *The Hero With a Thousand Faces* (Princeton, 1972) proved most valuable.

19. See the bibliography for works by Jan de Vries consulted for this study.

20. Vilhelm Grönbech's *Culture of the Teutons* (Oxford, 1931) is one of the most important works for this work. Although Grönbech's work in general may be somewhat outdated, his approach is very similar to that of a new breed of investigators such as P. Bauschatz, P. Buchholz, J. Fleck, and L. Gruber who,

although their conclusions may be quite divergent, nevertheless try to follow the general principle of viewing the material in question through the eyes of the culture which recorded, or created it.

21. See Ch. V.

22. This type of approach within the Gmc. tradition is suggested by the work of M. I. Steblin-Kamenskij in his *Saga Mind* (Odense Univ. Press, 1973), as well as by the "new breed" of investigators mentioned above in Note 20. The work of G. Dumézil, among others, has also contributed to this attitude toward archaic "literature," however, all investigators are by no means in agreement on this question.

23. The term "rite" is presented here in its broadest sense, of structured action toward a goal of a sacred or magical nature, and in some cases fictionalized reflections of such action.

24. For a discussion of the term "sacred" see R. Otto (1913), and for a more comprehensive view, see M. Eliade (1959), especially the introduction to this work.

CHAPTER TWO

REVIEW OF PREVIOUS SCHOLARSHIP

In the many years of continuous "*Nibelungenstudien*," countless volumes have been written concerning the legend of Sigurðr-Sigfrid and the Nibelungen. However, very little in-depth work has been devoted to the phase of Sigurðr's career which is discussed in the present work. Most scholars have been more intrigued with the dragon-slaying and the maid-awakening episodes. This is at once puzzling and at the same time understandable. It is puzzling in that the early segment of Sigurðr's life, spent under the tutelage of the dwarf-smith, is an integral part of the legend which appears in most versions of the story of Sigurd except the *NL*, and which is even prominently portrayed in the medieval artwork depicting Sigurðr from Norway to Spain. This reluctance is also understandable in that most scholars dealing with the Nibelungen material have made the reconciliation of the many variants an important part of their work, and this section certainly presents the most widely divergent aspect of the legend.

This state of affairs has made a review of previous scholarship concerning this phase of Sigurðr's career somewhat inconsistent, as there has not been a continuous, in-depth study of the dwarf-smith (*Vaterrache*) episode, at least not to the same extent as for the other segments of the saga. Karl Lachmann regarded this part of Sigurðr's life as taking place in a mythical world, and identified Reginn with the dwarf mentioned in the Vsp. 12. Also he considered Reginn to be a kind of "educator *par excellence*."[1] In 1879 Karl Müllenhoff devoted a study to *Sigurds Ahnen* in which he sheds some light on this phase of Sigurðr's heroic life, and its deeper meanings. Generally, he believes that the whole of the *Völsungasaga* is based upon Óðinic principles derived from the Istvaeonic, or Frankish cultic life and belief, and that the cult of the ancestors plays an important part in this belief structure. Müllenhoff emphasizes the role of Óðinn, and points to the uniqueness of the Völsung legend with regard to Óðinn's continuous activity throughout the saga. Perhaps most important for this present study is a statement which appears concerning the relationship between Sigurðr and Sigmundr: " ... *mit der Erzeugung Sigfrids aber hat Sigmund seine Bestimmung erfüllt.*"[2] Following the example of Karl Steiger, P. D. Chantepie

9

de la Saussaye considers Sigurðr to be a cosmological myth, and as such he prefers the version (cf. ÞS) which shows Sigurðr being reared in the forest.(3) No doubt as a symbol for the pre-dawn or pre-vernal darkness. Andreas Heusler in his study *Altnordische Dichtung und Prosa von Jung Sigurd*,(4) correctly indicates the close relationship between Sigurðr and Sigmundr, and he points out three major factors facilitating this connection: 1) the sword (Gramr), 2) the woman (Hjördís), and 3) the God (Óðinn). Óðinn aids both heroes throughout their careers, Hjördís is the wife of Sigmundr and the mother of Sigurðr, and the crux of the complex is the sword, Gramr. The sword was given by Óðinn to Sigmundr, and it was in effect "taken away" by him when he broke it with his spear, Gungnir. Then Hjördís becomes the agent by which the sword is preserved and given to Sigurðr.. Heusler sees the sword as a bearer of "*Schicksal*" and a gift from Óðinn. Franz Rolf Schröder considers Sigurðr to be a divine son archetype, and that the original form of the saga depicted him as a waif of latent royal qualities.(5)

Emil Ploss investigates the relationship between Sigurðr and Reginn on a moral and legalistic plane. He sees Sigurðr intimately related to Reginn through the institution of fosterage, and that this relationship brings Sigurðr into a close proximity with the *jötnaætt* and ultimately with Fáfnir, the brother of Reginn. But besides this Sigurðr-Reginn-Fáfnir complex, and the legalistic problems which Reginn faces as the result of his plot to kill his brother, Ploss also finds an interesting socio-legal aspect to the relationship between Sigurðr and Reginn, between the warrior and the smith. This relationship is characterized by the *Rechtsunfähigkeit* of the smith, and his use of the warrior to gain vengeance for wrongs done to him.(6)

In his rather folkloristic study, Friedrich Panzer provides an interesting parallel to the acquisition of Gramr, which he finds in the *Nibelungenlied*. This is the *Schwertleite* of the second *Âvintiure*, in which the pagan mytho-cultic motifs have been replaced by the elegant, chivalric ritual of the *Schwertleite*.(7)

All of these studies shed some light on various aspects of this phase of Sigurðr's early life and education under Reginn, however, it is hoped that the present work will provide an in-depth investigation of this segment of the saga, at least of the version found in the *VS-CR* redaction.

A review of the previous scholarship concerning the ideology of Germanic rebirth provides us with a far more consistent and historically verifiable picture. In 1855 Konrad Maurer first suggested the possibility of a connection between the belief in rebirth and Old Norse naming customs.(8) Then Kristian Kålund further developed this idea and noted that the people would name their children after an ancestor or a relative whom the child most resembled. Kålund thought that this practice served to celebrate and to continue inherited familial characteristics, and in a way to transfer the "luck" of the earlier name-holder to the new family member.(9) Thus by 1879 the basic foundations for studies in the Germanic belief in rebirth had already been laid, and the scholarship which was to follow can essentially be viewed as an elaboration and a refinement of Kålund's ideas.

The first great elaboration came in 1893 in an article by Gustav Storm called "Vore Forfædres Tro paa Sjælevandring og deres Opkaldesesystem."(10) This article is actually the most radical of all the studies concerning the Germanic doctrine of rebirth. It suggests that we are dealing with a true *Seelenwanderung*, although it does not suggest that this soul is the same as the personality, it does promote the idea of an immortality of the soul. Roughly formulated, Storm's theory states that rebirth equals a transmigration of souls and that this transmigration is virtually indistinguishable from the practice of *Nachbenennung*. The name equals the soul, and the transfer of the name equals the transfer of the soul, however, this can only be the case when the name of a deceased ancestor is involved. Thus, for Storm, the inauguration of the practice of naming children after living relatives spelled the end of the belief in true rebirth, i.e., *Sjælevandring*. For a period of approximately twenty years Storm's views held a virtually unchallenged position among scholars who approached the problem. H. Gering,(11) A. Olrik,(12) and B. Kahle(13) all more or less defend Storm's ideas in various contexts.

W. v. Unwerth believed that the Lapps introduced the concept of rebirth in Norway, and that this ideology soon assimilated to the Germanic naming customs.(14) Other scholars including H. Naumann,(15) F. Niedner,(16) and B. Nerman(17) generally continue along the pattern outlined by Kålund and Storm without much elaboration. In 1925 G. Neckel suggested that the inheritance of personal characteristics was spoken of as a rebirth, and that this phenomenon coupled with the naming practices illustrated a high

11

development of ancestral pride among the Germanic peoples.(18) The next year (1926) Karl Helm also outlined some ideas concerning rebirth in Germanic tradition, but this study generally adds nothing new to the discussion.(19)

Max Keil summarized and criticized the studies discussed above in his work *Altisländische Namenwahl* (1931)(20) and he suggested that the Nachbenennung did not equal rebirth. Keil more correctly connected the naming practices with the belief in the *hamingja* and/or *fylgja*, and the transferability of these concepts from one person to another. According to his conception it is the act (rite) of name-giving and not the name itself which transfers the essence of "luck" (*hamingja*). He does not doubt the existence of a Germanic belief in rebirth, but rather he questions the causal relationship between this phenomenon and the practice of *Nachbenennung*. Keil's study represents the best refinement of the theories outlined by previous scholars and he paved the way for a more detailed examination of the connections between naming, rebirth, and the aspects of the psychosomatic complex.

In 1937 Karl August Eckhardt's landmark work, *Irdische Unsterblichkeit: Germanischer Glaube an die Wiederverkörperung in der Sippe*(21) appeared, and it has remained "the major text" on the subject of Germanic rebirth, or *Wiederverkörperung*. Although in many respects Max Keil's study is superior to *Irdische Unsterblichkeit*, especially where questions concerning the role of the *hamingja-fylgja* aspects are involved, Eckhardt does bring an enormous body of evidence to bear on the problem of rebirth from all realms of the Germanic world, as well as from the larger Indo-European sphere. Eckhardt's work generally represents a return to the views held by G. Storm *et al.* concerning the relationship between *Namengebung* and *Wiederverkörperung*, and at the same time he looks for the origins of this belief within the Indo-European tradition. In the 1956 edition of his *Altgermanische Religionsgeschichte*(22) Jan de Vries supports the conclusions of Eckhardt while re-emphasizing the Indo-European aspect.

Chapter V of the present work presents an outline of the belief in rebirth coupled with the functions of the various soul conceptions found among the North Germanic peoples during the latter portion of the heathen period.(23) However, this discussion is not the core of this thesis, but rather it should only serve as supporting material for conclusions reached in the interpretive portion of the work. It is rather safe to say that evidence for the belief in rebirth among the ancient Germanic peoples, in one form or another, has been well established by a large number of modern scholars, and that we may follow the trails which they blazed in order to come to deeper realizations concerning Germanic religious belief in these areas in question.

Footnotes to Chapter Two

1. K. Lachmann (1829), 45.
2. K. Müllenhoff (1879(, 144.
3. P. D. C. de la Saussaye (1902), 144.
4. A. Heusler (1919), 174 ff.
5. F. R. Schröder (1919), 8 ff.
6. E. Ploss (1966), 29-30.
7. Fr. Panzer (1955), 288-289.
8. K. Maurer (1855), I, 234.
9. K. Kålund (1879), 276-278.
10. G. Storm (1893), 199 ff. Storm was evidently influenced to some degree by the theories of E. Tylor (cf. E. Tylor, *Primitive Culture* [London: John Murray, 1871]). Tylor's theories were formulated from the perspective of the soul-concept, and he also showed a lively interest in the subject of soul-transmigration. It is therefore not surprising to find his ideas appearing in works concerning the similar Gmc. phenomena. However, the Gmc. evidence did not completely lend itself to an animistic interpretation, although entities such as the *fylgja* were consistently interpreted in an animistic framework. The theories of R. H. Codrington concerning *mana*, which were initially developed after a study of Polynesian evidence, were in many respects more applicable to certain aspects of the Gmc. belief in souls and in rebirth. (Cf. R. H. Codrington, *The Melanesians: Studies in Their Anthropology and Folklore* [Oxford: Clarendon Press, 1891].)
11. H. Gering, ed. (1897), 29. *Eyrbyggja saga*. A note on ch. 12;4 states: "*es hängt diese sitte mit dem uralten glauben an die seelenwanderung zusammen: man nahm an, dass die seele des verstorbenen in den körper des neugeborenen kindes übergehe.*"
12. A. Olrik (1890), 17, states: "*Ein eigenartiger Ausdruck des Geschlechtszusammenhanges liegt darin, dass man glaubte, der kürzlich Verstorbene werde in den Nachkommen wiedergeboren.*"
13. B. Kahle (1910), 142 ff.
14. These views are to be found in two works, w. v. Unwerth (1911), 37, and W. v. Unwerth (1913), 179-187.
15. H. Naumann (1912), 164-167.
16. F. Niedner (1913) , 66.
17. B. Nerman. (1917).
18. G. Neckel (1925), 33. Views expressed in this period, and following, were to some extent influenced by the sociological, structuralist approaches exemplified by E. Durkheim. Cf. E. Durkheim, *Les formes elementaries de la vie religieuse: Le systeme totemigue en Australie* (Paris: F. Alcan, 1912). A van Gennep had already provided a synthesis of the animistic and dynamistic theories in his *Les Rites de Passage* (Paris: E. Nourry, 1909).
19. K. Helm (1926), 359 ff.
20. M. Keil (1931), 104 ff. Keil seems to have synthesized the various views of scholars in both the anthropological-religious historical schools, as well as those

within the literary field. Keil's result is more dynamistic when compared to that of Storm. However, it is again important to note that animism never dominated the theories of Gmc. rebirth.

21. K. A. Eckhardt (1937). The views of Eckhardt are more fully discussed in Chapters V and VII.

22. J. de Vries (1956), I, 217 ff.

23. As noted in Chapter I, it is realized that we are not dealing with pure heathen texts, however, we are in most cases working with texts which are relatively unspoiled by overt Christian thought either by virtue of unprejudiced or zealously antiquarian editors or by the intentional archaizing tendencies among some of these editors. That is, concerning this last point, some ancient editors reported on heathen practices and beliefs which they apparently no longer practiced or believed, but which they knew to have been practiced and believed by the people of the heathen period, e.g., the editor of the last segment of HHII (cf. the prose concluding that lay) and the editor of the *VS*.

CHAPTER THREE

OUTLINE OF TEXTUAL SOURCES

Generally, the following represents an attempt to outline the major Nordic texts dealing with the initial phase of Young-Sigurðr's heroic career, plus an effort to determine, in broad terms, the point(s) of origin for the Sigurðr-myth, and the area of distribution for this "proto-saga." Also the mode by which the saga entered the West-Norse cultural sphere will be considered briefly.

During the latter half of the 20th-century it was fairly well established that the story of Sigurðr, and heroic literature in general, was first orally formulated in prose and then it migrated into the various Germanic regions, primarily in prose(1) and only secondarily in poetic compositions.(2) A. Heusler's *Liedertheorie* dominated views concerning northern heroic literature until the middle of the 20th-century. Heusler contended that Germanic heroic literature was first composed by wandering *scopes* in poetic, lyrical form and that the *scopes* would perform these songs in chieftains' halls during feasts and celebrations. Heusler also believed that these songs originated in the southern Germanic territory, among the Goths (5th-8th-centuries CE), the Franks and the Anglo-Saxons, and then spread northward with the wanderings of the *scopes*. He also maintained that Denmark, Norway, and Sweden contributed very little to Germanic literature before 1200 CE.(3) Concerning the Sigurðr-literature, Heusler of course contended that it was originally a series of non-biographical poetic works originating in the south.(4)

These views drew an energetic attack from the Swedish scholar Fritz Askeberg, who challenged Heusler's findings as *"alltför romantisk."* Askeberg's ideas rest upon a foundation of what was, in 1944, a fairly revolutionary premise, namely that the northern region (Sweden, the Baltic coast, Denmark, the North Sea coast, and Norway) was the area of strongest Germanic cultural concentration, from which important cultural features such as legend, poetry and the runes,(5) spread southward. These arguments are supported by the evidence that most *Fornaldarsögur* take place in Norway, Gotland, eastern Sweden, Russia, etc., but rarely in the west or south.(6) For Askeberg the heroic literature is an indigenous Germanic development, that has its roots in the age preceding the migration period. As far as the story of Sigurðr and the *Niflungasaga* are concerned, Askeberg is unable to account for all the historical, southern material which appears in the latter part of this complex. However, he is quick to point out the distinction between Sigurðr's youthful exploits (which are extremely well developed in the northern tradition, but corrupt and incomplete in the southern tradition, i.e., the *NL*), and the episodes which follow these adventures, which are of a simi-historical nature. Furthermore, Askeberg indicates many elements retained in the *NL* which he believes betray a northern origin, e.g., Sîfrîd's home in the Netherlands, Brünhild's origin in Iceland, and the occurrence of Liudegast of Denmark.(7) Here, Askeberg recognizes the archaic and mythic nature of the initial episodes in the life of Young-Sigurðr.

The Swedish scholar also maintains, contrary to Heusler, that the original form of heroic literature was probably prose, which migrated southward with the various Germanic tribes, and which was passed orally from generation to generation in an outwardly flexible form, but with firmly fixed motifs and themes. According to Askeberg, the *Fornaldarsögur* were formed with the intention of containing the knowledge which posterity believed itself to have about ancient times.(8) He is eager to indicate that Scandinavia is also the homeland for heroic poetry insofar as style and form are concerned.(9) That is, that they remain essentially unaffected by classical forms.

If we accept these arguments, then it is clear that the root motifs of Germanic heroic legend began to be formed in the first two centuries of the Common Era, along the coast of the Baltic Sea, in southern Sweden and in adjacent regions. It seems advisable to draw some distinction between these oral root motifs upon which the legends were built, and the final narrative forms which we now have in written monuments. These oral motifs could remain fairly consistent and fixed(10) while the language, and superficial circumstances could change quite freely. In this thesis we are more interested in the paradigmatic motifs, themes, and archetypal figures rather than textual mechanics. These motifs usually remain internally sound, however, they are often the subject of redistribution. The various versions of the *Sigurðarsaga* provide examples of both situations, as this chapter is intended to demonstrate.(11)

The central motif of the story of Sigurðr is the dragon-slaying and subsequent acquisition of the gold hoard. This, and various other motifs of the saga are portrayed in texts, inscriptions and carvings which predate the oldest continuous text dealing with Sigurðr (the

Reginsmál-Fáfnismál-Sigrdrífumál complex in the *CR* ca. 1000 CE) by as much as three centuries. We find early written evidence for the *Sigurðarsaga* in three bodies of literature, the OE *Bēowulf*, the Old Norse *CR*, and in some Old Norse Skaldic poetry. In *Bēowulf* lines 875-902 (from ca. 700 CE) a *scop* sings a panegyric lay to the hero in which he portrays the dragon-slaying motif, in this case transferred to Sigmundr. In the earliest stage of the saga the names Völsi, Völsung, Sigmundr, and perhaps Sigurðr were in a confused state, the first three of these are attested alternate names, or *heiti*, for Óðinn.(12) Here, it is interesting to note the highly developed state of the story of Sigmundr and its correspondences with the version found six centuries later in the *Völsungasaga*, not only the dragon-slaying and treasure-taking but also Sigmundr's adventures with Sinfjötli (OE Fitela), and the names Völsi (OE Wæls), and Völsungr (OE Wælsing) are mentioned. J. de Vries is inclined to believe that these lines have a North Germanic source.(13)

Two of the oldest Eddic lays also contain references to the story of Sigurðr. The "Völundarkviða," which dates from the latter half of the 9th-century, and which was probably composed in Norway, contains the following lines:

> *Gull var þar eigi   á Grana leiðo*
> *fiarri hugða ec várt land   fiǫllom Rínar. . .*

(Gold was not there on Grains path I think our land is far from the mountains of the Rhine. . .) [Vkv. 14. 1-4.]

This is a clear representation of the way in which Sigurðr took the gold and of the place where this act occurred. The location is also cited in the "Atlakviða," also from late 9th-century Norway, where we find:

> *Vǫll léz ycr oc mundo gefa   víðrar Gnitaheiðar*

(He says he will give you the   field [Neckel] or gold [Bugge] *of* wide Gnita-heath) [Atk. 5, 1-2.]

There are three Skaldic poems which refer to the story of Sigurðr, however, the "Bjarkamál" sts. 5-6 are late (12th-century) interpolations. In a poem about Haraldr Blátönn, the Skald Einarr Helgason wrote in 985 CE:

19

1. *Liðbrǫndum kná Lundar*   The land-valiant warrior of Lund
   1 andfrœkn jǫfurr granda. is able to be generous.
   Hykka rœsis rekka   I do not think the warrior lacks
   Rínar grjót of þrjóta   the pebbles of the Rhine.

[Kock., I, 65]

Later, but perhaps before the appearance of the Reginsmál-Fáfnismál complex, the Skald Þórmóðr Bersason wrote, ca. 1024-27:

Loftungu gaft lengi   You gave praise (-tongue) for a
                        long time
látr, þats Fáfnir átti.   for the "litter" (=gold) which
                        Fáfnir owned.

[Kock., I, 135]

Besides these documents, there also exists a body of plastic art (already briefly mentioned in Chapter I, note 2) which attests to the early wide, and "deep" distribution of the legend.(14) The oldest of the monuments is a group of crosses on the Isle of Man, which were carved by Norwegian Vikings during the latter part of the 10th-century. The Malew and Jurby crosses portray the slaying of Fáfnir, while the Andreas church monument adds the heart-eating, and Maughold portrays Loki slaying Otr, the heart-eating, and Grani with the treasure. Also from approximately the same period, we find the Halton Cross in Lancashire, England, which was also carved by Norwegians. This monument depicts Reginn forging Gramr, the heart-eating, the reception of second-sight by Sigurðr, and it also represents a horse, Grani(?).

Other monuments which attest to the phase of Sigurðr's career in question here are found in the artwork of Norwegian churches dating from the 11th- to 13th-centuries. The portals of the churches of Hallestad and Veigusdal show the forging and testing of Gramr, (Veigusdal includes Grani) while the portal of Lardal church depicts the wergeld of Otr and the forging of Gramr. The Cathedral of San Guesa in Navarra, Spain, also portrays the smith, Reginn.(15) The Swedish Ockelbo-stone contains an interesting representation which is of some importance to this thesis. This stone, definitely a Sigurðr-inscription with a clear depiction of the worm-slaying, portrays two men at a gaming table. Could this be Sigurðr and Reginn during Sigurðr's period of education?(16) There are a number of other carvings and stones which depict various motifs from the *Siguðarsaga*, all of this indicates a well developed mythology, at least as early as 1000, that is as far as certain motifs (e.g., Otr-ransom, Gramr-forging, Grani dragon-slaying, heart-eating, and second-sight) are concerned.

Most of the more recent scholars are inclined to believe that a highly developed legend about Sigurðr entered the West-Norse cultural sphere during the latter half of the 10th-century,(17) however, this is not to say that the various motifs and heroic paradigms were not already found in this region to some degree. It is by no means certain when the story of Sigurðr became connected with the *Niflungasaga*,(18) nor is it certain at which point, if ever, the saga existed in oral tradition in a form approximating that of the *Völsungasaga*. It is hoped that this thesis will be able to demonstrate the possibility (through religious and cultural contexts) of an arrangement of motifs similar to that found in the *VS-CR* version, at least for the segment of the saga in question. No one doubts the existence of an oral tradition, and archeological, cultural, and textual evidence supports this contention. P. Buchholz is inclined to believe that the *fornaldarsaga* would be incomprehensible without presupposing a long history of oral tradition.(22)

The general concept, and probability of an oral tradition is important to the establishment of an old mythological framework, but an examination of the extant texts is the main purpose of this chapter. The following sections briefly survey the major Nordic texts concerning this phase of the Sigurðr legend

Codex Regius (CR)

Within the *CR* we are principally concerned with two lays: the "Reginsmál" and the "Grípisspá" The "Reginsmál" dates from just before 1000, while the "Grípisspá" was probably one of the youngest lays included in the *CR*, which was compiled around 1270.(23) The "Grípisspá" directly precedes the "Reginsmál" in the manuscript of the *CR*, however, it is probable that the chronological position of the "Grípisspá" would be somewhere within the sequence of events outlined in the "Reginsmál," since from the content of the "Grípisspá" it is clear that Sigurðr has not avenged Sigmundr, yet he already possesses Grani. The *Völsungasaga* places the prophecy of Grípir after the forging of Gramr and before the *Vaterrache*. Essentially, the "Grípisspá" is a summary of the story of Sigurðr, in

21

which all the events of Sigurðr's life are outlined from the avenging of Sigmundr to Sigurðr's death. The "Reginsmál" begins with a prose section which first tells of Sigurðr's choosing of Grani, and then introduces Reginn as Sigurðr's *fóstri*. Reginn tells Sigurðr the story of Andvari's hoard,(24) and then he eggs Sigurðr to kill Fáfnir and take the gold. However, the hero knows that he must first avenge his father, and so they set out toward *Hundingaland* aboard longships in order to complete the required deed of vengeance. Along the way they are hailed by a mysterious stranger who asks to come on board. This granted, the stranger, Hnikarr (= Óðinn), imparts some war-wisdom to Sigurðr. There follows a single stanza which indicates the completed vengeance of Sigurðr.

R. Harris believes that the Grípisspá should be understood totally outside the structural framework of the rest of the story of Sigurðr, as an artistic synopsis of that legend, created for a specific audience. Most of the artistry which Harris cites in connection with the Grípisspá concerns its careful use of form and structure.(25) It is also possible that the idea of the prophecy of Sigurðr's *móðirbróðir* was an expected part of any proto-saga. One of the more curious characteristics of the Grípisspá is the fact that Sigurðr anticipates the prophecies of Grípir as the hero eggs his uncle on to foretell more of the future. Could this perhaps indicate a poetic treatment of older prose material?(26) Another interesting question must also be asked concerning the origin of this prophecy in the Sigurðr-literature: Did the prophecy of Grípir exist in the proto-*Sigurðarsaga*, and then find its way into the *VS* through the *CR*? Dr did it occur independently in both works?(27)

The "Reginsmál" along with two other Eddic lays, the "Fáfnismál" and the "Sigdrífumál," form a poetic trilogy outlining the early life of Sigurðr Fáfnisbani. J. de Vries, along with many other scholars, considers this complex to be an interpolation into a previously developed prose structure. He maintains that the oldest part of this lay is the *Vaterrache* segment in *fornyrðislag* (11th-century).(28) A. Heusler wants to divide the "Reginsmál" into two parts, one in *ljóðaháttr* and the other in *fornyrðislag*, and then connect the *ljóðaháttr* segment with the "Fáfnismál" to form a "*Lied vom Drachenhort.*" The remaining strophes of the "Reginsmál" in *fornyrðislag* would then be known as the "*Lied von Sigurds Vaterrache.*"(29) Heusler also indicates a northern origin for the *Vaterrache* theme.(30) The death of Sigmundr is not explicitly recorded in the *CR*, however, his death is presupposed in the content of both the "Grípisspá" and "Reginsmál." This may serve as an indicator of the magnitude of this tradition, which is implicit in the Eddic material. S. Gutenbrunner suspects that the *Spruchdichtung* contained in the "Reginsmál" is older than the lay itself, and that it was extracted from common tradition, and included in the lay in order to more fully develop the education of the hero.(31) If this is true it would only add to the value of the "Reginsmál" as a source for the history of Germanic religion and mythology.

This inclusion of older didactic material is also indicative of the consistent tendency to make the Sigurðr-lays a record of the education of the ideal, archetypal, heroic youth. Furthermore, whenever two figures speak to one another, moralistic observations are inserted, to reinforce this teaching tradition.(32)

There appears to have been a general tendency to string together more motifs in order to create more elaborate sagas, and to relate more heroes to one another in an effort to create more complex and widespread interdependent relationships. An important question to ask in this regard is: How is this connection accomplished? H. Kuhn rightly notes the uniqueness of the Young-Sigurðr poetry in comparison to other Old Norse poetry which is supposed to derive from southern Germanic tradition. He also ventures an opinion that it is through the *Vaterrache* motif that Sigurðr becomes connected to Völsungar.(33) Regardless of whether these observations are accurate or not, it is probably true that this would have been a likely and valid method to connect two cycles.(34)

These lays of the Elder Edda form a primary source for the study of the heroic career of Young-Sigurðr. The validity of this source for purposes of this thesis is reinforced by the fact that the *Völsungasaga* contains no major contradictions for the portion of the saga in question here.

Völsungasaga

The redaction in which we now have the *Völsunga saga* must date from between 1250 and 1260 because of the use of material from the *Þiðreks saga* which may be firmly dated at that time.(35) However, since this redaction is probably a later reworking of older material paraphrased from Eddic lays, this later interpolation is not a good criterion for dating the older form of the *Völsungasaga*.(36) Also the connecting of Hákon Hákonarson (1217-63) to the composition through his ancestor Ragnar Loðbrók (who is said to have married Áslaug Sigurðardóttir) is a poor criterion for dating because this too was probably a later interpolation.(37) All of this serves to push the date of the proto-*VS* back as far as the year 1200, however, the actual form in which we now have the saga may be as recent as 1270.(38) J. de Vries speculates that because of the identical ordering of events in the *CR* and in the *VS,* they are contemporaries.(39) This may also be due to the nature of the underlying tradition.

R. Finch speculates that the sagaman of the *Völsungasaga* used a *Liederbuch* other than the *CR* itself as a source for portions of his manuscript, because the *Völsungasaga* gives complete readings for defective portions of the *CR* manuscript.(40) An Icelandic origin for the *Völsungasaga* is most probable, as a result of the demonstrated access to known Icelandic sources.(41) However, D. A. Seip believes that the ultimate source of the *Völsungasaga* may have been Norwegian.(42)

For a detailed description of the events portrayed in the *Völsungasaga*, see Chapter IV of this work.

The *Völsungasaga* is the major source of material for this thesis. It is hoped that this, and the following chapter, coupled with parallel material found elsewhere, will provide enough evidence to demonstrate that the *Völsungasaga* is indeed a reliable source of information in the field of pre-Christian Germanic religion and culture.

Edda Snorra Sturlusonar

The date of Snorri's composition of the Edda is quite firmly established at 1222 CE.(43) The *ESS* is extant in four manuscripts: the *Codex Regius* (*CR*), the *Codex Wormianus* (*CW*), which is missing chapters 39-43 including the section in which we are interested, the *Codex Uppsaliensis* (*CU*), and a paper manuscript, the *Codex Trajectinus* (*CT*). Although the *CR, CW* and *CT* are more closely related and perhaps give a better representation of the original version written by Snorri, the *CU* is generally older and gives a better reading in some passages where the *CR, CW,* or *CT* manuscripts are defective.(44) Various copyists, in a variety of locations, probably created versions in accordance with the needs of those making use of the book.

The portion of the *ESS* in question (chapter 40 of the *Skáldskaparmál*) is principally concerned with the *otrgjöld* and recovery of the ransom by Sigurðr, and therefore it is the least detailed of our texts with regard to matters peripheral to this central theme. It is said that Reginn was with king Hjálprekr as a smith, and that he took Sigurðr, the son of Sigmundr Völsungarson, into fosterage. Sigurðr is described as ". . . ágætastr allra herkonunga af ætt ok afli ok hug. . ." Reginn tells Sigurðr about the gold and eggs him to win it. To this end, the smith fashions a sword called Gramr, and Sigurðr tests the sword by cutting a flock of wool against a stream, and by splitting Reginn's anvil. From this point the narrative proceeds directly to the slaying of Fáfnir. Later, the name of Sigurðr's horse, Grani, is mentioned.

The most striking characteristic of this sequence of events is the absence of the *Vaterrache* episode. This is not altogether surprising since this would interrupt the continuity of the narrative. Sigmundr is only mentioned twice in the *ESS*, both times in the *Skáldskaparmál*. The first time he is mentioned as the father of Sigurðr, but later the story of Sigmundr and Sinfjötli is related where it is stated that both heroes could withstand poison on their skins, but that only Sigmundr could drink it and not be harmed.(45) The *ESS* is a valuable source of supporting evidence when it treats the motif in question, however, it is so often concerned with its own special purposes that it sometimes passes over certain details.

Nornagests þáttr

This *þáttr* belongs to the decedent period of Icelandic literature in the 14th-century, at least not before 1300.(46) The text appears in the *Flateyjarbók*(47) and the writer was probably familiar with both the *CR* and the *VS*, since the *þáttr* follows the saga quite closely.(48)

The events of the *Nornagests þáttr* do not contradict the *CR-VS* version, but the author choose to emphasize certain aspects, since the events are seen through the eyes of the wanderer. Norna-Gestr comes to the court of King Hjálprekr and becomes a servant to Sigurðr. They go to the house of Reginn, the smith, who was Sigurðr's tutor, and who had taught Sigurðr all about his ancestors, among other things. While at Reginn's dwelling they learn of Fáfnir, and Reginn forges the sword, Gramr, which Sigurðr tests by cutting wool in the Rhine and splitting Reginn's anvil. Reginn eggs Sigurðr to kill Fáfnir rather than avenge his father and grandfather, but Sigurðr is steadfast and gathers an army to avenge Sigmundr and Eylimi. He sets out across the sea with Reginn, Hámundr (his brother), and Norna-Gestr among his army to fight with the three Sons of Hundingr, Lyngvi, Álfr, and Hemingr. Here, the most curious passage in this segment of the *Nornagests þáttr* appears, in which Siguröïr borrows Reginn's sword, Riðill, and in exchange promises to kill Fáfnir when they return from the expedition.(49) Then a storm, which was raised by the magic of the Hundingssynir, begins and Siguröïr's ships sail closer to shore. There they see the *heklumaðr* Hnikarr (= Óðinn) on a rocky crag and he asks to come on board. (This whole section follows the *CR*.) The storm ceases and Hnikarr imparts his war-wisdom. When they land in Hundingaland, Siguröïr (with Gramr, not Riðill) leads his army against that of the Hundingssynir. By nightfall all of the sons of King Hundingr and their men were dead, except for Lyngvi, their leader, who had been captured. As the next day dawns, Hnikarr disappears.(50) The *blóðugr örn* ("blood-eagle") is carved on Lyngvi, and he dies with great bravery.

    J. de Vries points out that the *Nornagests þáttr* was most probably inspired by the Greek Meleagros-legend,(51) and he also indicates the contrast in mood between the *Völsungasaga* and the *þáttr*. The *Völsungasaga* is a product of the heathen age, and is taken quite seriously, while the story of Norna-Gestr belongs to a decedent period full of foreign influences.(52) L. L. M. Hollander sees many of the attributes of Óðinn in the character of Norna-Gestr. However, Norna-Gestr is not a hypostasis of Óðinn, but rather he seems to be a literary product which was greatly shaped by ideas surrounding Óðinn. In fact, the heroes mentioned in the *þáttr* are for the most part Óðinic.(53) This would seem to be further evidence of the Óðinic presence which permeates the whole legend of Siguröïr. The *Nornagests þáttr* is a valuable source because it demonstrates the fundamental, internal integrity of the legend of Siguröïr, and it is especially noteworthy for this work because it places heavy emphasis upon the *Vaterrache*. Also the above mentioned Óðinic element is extremely strong in this *þáttr*, much of which may be pure literary invention. Even allowing for this literary element, the essence of Óðinic presence is essentially pagan, and this in spite of patently Christian setting of the *þáttr*.

Regin smiður

    Perhaps the most remarkable aspect of this text is the high state of internal integrity which it was able to maintain over a period of several centuries, transmitted orally, until it was first written down in

the late 18th-century. The ballad tradition could have begun in the Faeroes as early as the late 13th- or early 14th-century, probably brought to the islands from Denmark, where this tradition was in its *Blütezeit* during this period. The Danish tradition declined with the waning of the Middle Ages, but the conservative Faeroes continued in
their old ways.(54) As the following outline of events will show, the correspondence between these ballads and the *CR-VS* version of the Sigurðr-legend is very striking. After being pierced with poison swords (a departure from the tradition found elsewhere of Sigmundur's immunity to venom) Sigmundur's sword is broken and he lays dying, a victim of the Hundingar. Hjørdis comes to Sigmundur. He then foretells the greatness of his son Sjúrður (Sigurðr) and how the young hero will avenge his father's death with the broken sword. Sigmundur instructs Hjørdis to go to Regin the smith in order to have the sword reforged. The hero dies at night, and is buried. Hjørdis goes to King Hjálprek and marries him. Sjúrður is born, and at once fostered to Hjálprek, where he grows fast and learns the martial arts. One day while Sjúrður is engaged in a conflict with the swains in Hjálprek's court, they confront him with his father's unavenged death, and they chide him for not avenging this deed. Sjúrður goes to his mother and learns of his ancestry and receives the broken sword and the byrnie of Sigmundur. Hjørdis tells her son to go to Regin to have the blade reforged. But she also speaks of Fáfnir and says to beware of Regin. Then Hjørdis instructs Sjúrður on the method he is to use in the choosing of his horse, Grani.(55) After the young hero obtains his steed, he rides to the abode of the smith, Regin. There, Sjúrður asks Regin to reforge the sword, and twice Regin attempts the process, without success. But on the third try he is successful. Sjúrður tests the blade by splitting the anvil,(56) and then goes out and avenges his father by slaying the sons of Hunding.

E. M. Smith-Dampier states that the Faeroese ballads are essentially Norse in tone and atmosphere, yet he also maintains that they resemble the German versions more than the Nordic ones.(57) An archaic "supernatural" ambiance pervades the whole *Regin smiður*, and although Óðinn plays a smaller role in this text he is still prominent as an advisor before the slaying of Fáfnir.

This text is extremely valuable as supporting material for the mythological validity of the northern branch of the Sigurðr-tradition (as found in the *CR-VS* version). The study of the Faeroese ballads present many more complex problems than we may enter into at present, however, what is of primary importance here, is the evidence of a stable tradition rooted in the heroic heathen period indicated by this text.

Þiðrekssaga af Bern

This saga is ostensibly about the court of Thedoric the Great, the 6th-century Ostrogothic king in Ravenna, Italy. The *ÞS* may be firmly dated at ca. 1250, during the reign of Hákon Hákonarson, who promoted the collection of such sagas. The place of writing was probably Bergen, Norway.(58) Although the original redaction, upon which all extant MSS are based, was produced in Bergen, that MS was most certainly based upon a Low-German, probably Saxon, exemplar.(59) This exemplar would have come north along the sea-trading routes which were strongly developed between Saxony and that region of Norway. The problems surrounding the manuscripts of the *Þiðrekssaga* are quite complex,(60) however, a brief survey of the major manuscripts may demonstrate the distribution of the *ÞS* material. The Stockholm membran (Mb) dates from the end of the 13th-century, and although it is the oldest manuscript, it is not certain that it represents a version more faithful to the Bergen archetype than the other manuscripts.(61) There also exist two Icelandic paper manuscripts, A and B, which are closely related to one another, but which diverge substantially from the Mb. Both A and B date from the 17th-century. Interestingly, we also find two MSS representing Swedish translations (= Sv.) of the *ÞS*, which date from a little before 1448. These manuscripts indicate that the Þiðrekr-material was quite popular, among the Swedes at least. Generally, it seems reasonable to conclude that the *ÞS* represents a translation (and revision?) of a Low-German (Saxon) prose text concerning Dietrich von Bern and the various heroes associated with him, with countless later interpolations.

An examination of the events contained within the segment of the ˉin which we are interested (chapters 161-168) will reveal a remarkable contrast to the relatively consistent picture we perceive in the previously discussed texts, which together generally form what may be referred to as a "northern tradition."(62) Þiðrekr believes he has been betrayed by Sisibe and he orders her to be killed. The two men escorting her begin to fight over whether or not to kill her, and during the ensuing battle Sisibe gives birth to Sigurðr and places the baby in a glass container. As one of the men falls, he kicks the flask into a river and it rushes downstream. Upon seeing this, the queen dies. The glass container floats until it comes to a rocky shore, where it breaks and the child is nursed by hinds in the forest for twelve months. In this time he grows to the size of a four-year-old. Then Mimir the smith finds the child while wandering in the woods. The smith takes the boy as a *fóstri* and tries to teach him the smith's art and craft. But Sigurðr (or Sigfriðr) plays havoc with Mimir's apprentices, constantly bullying them, until one day Sigurðr goes too far by roughing up Æckiharð for hitting him with the tongs. To teach Sigurðr a lesson, Mimir sets him to work at the forge, but when the young hero strikes the iron, the anvil is driven into the ground and the tools and iron shatter. Sigurðr then runs and hides in his foster-mother's bower.

It is difficult to determine which of the two variants is older, however, the *ÞS* is definitely inferior to the *CR-VS* version with respect to its internal integrity and mythological authenticity. Although the initial segment describing Sigurðr's nurturing among the hinds appears archaic, it could be the result of classical influence. The divergence of the names of the brothers Reginn and Fáfnir (*CR-VS*, etc.) or Mimir and Reginn (*ÞS*) also presents an interesting and revealing contrast. The names in the *CR-VS* version seem to reflect their functions in the saga much more closely. "Reginn" probably means "advisor" or "powerful one,"(63) while "Fáfnir" may indicate "he who surrounds with his arms".(64) The name "Mimir' is probably connected to the concepts "to think over", or "to remember".(65) The Mimir/Reginn alternation is not that disturbing, however, the Reginn/Fáfnir confusion seems untenable.

The *ÞS* is interesting for this thesis from a contrastive standpoint. Instead of reinforcing the validity of the *CR-VS* version of the legend, it introduces a variant from a foreign source which describes a sequence of events quite different from the northern version. It is interesting to note that the *ÞS* also reflects the basic overall structure of the Young-Sigurðr myth in agreement with the *CR-VS* tradition as: fosterage (to a smith)—dragon-slaying—meeting with Brynhildr/Sigrdrífa.

It is hoped that this brief survey of textual sources and ideas underlying oral traditions will help toward the establishment of the mythological authenticity, the cultural authority and the internal integrity of the sources in question through a demonstration of their age, "depth," wide geographical distribution, and generally consistent paradigmatic qualities. This evidence is of course primarily valid for the time period between ca. 1000 and 1250 (*die Erzählzeit*) in the Norwegian-Icelandic cultural sphere. But we may also hope that it to some degree accurately reflects the values and institutions of the *fornöld (die Erzähltezeit)*, in the sense that these works are bound by the *laws of possibility*. These documents are not "mere flights of fancy," but rather they are governed by what the sagaman, and ultimately his audience knew to be possible—depending upon the laws which were thought to rule in the time in which the saga was set.(66) These problems are not central to this thesis, as we are less interested in literary questions than in the mythological and religious evidence which these texts may reveal.

Footnotes to Chapter Three

1. Cf. F. Askeberg (1944), 96-97, J. de Vries (1957), I, 88 ff., H. K u h n (1950), 33 ff., and S. Einarsson (1957), 35.

2. Eddic poetry from Norway to Iceland, see also the discussion of the Vkv. and Akv.

3. A. Heusler (1923), 2-4; 109-119.

4. A. Heusler (1919), 162.

5. Askeberg believes that the runes originated, or came into use, among the Goths in the 1st- and 2nd-centuries of the Common Era, while those people were inhabiting the Baltic coast. The fact that these cultural features are found in their greatest concentration in the north is also an important, and logical, aspect of Askeberg's argument.

6. H. Schück (1933, I, 212 ff.

7. F. Askeberg (1944), 95-97; 104. Askeberg's views have generally been accepted, even by Heusler's students. Cf. H. Kuhn (1950), 30 ff. and J. de Vries (1957), I, 88-89.

8. F. Askeberg (1944), 104-105. Askeberg maintains that so-called *Vikingasögur* are modernizations of older sagas, and that the Viking Age is not the normal background for the *Fornaldarsögur*. Cf. also P. Buchholz (1977), 126 ff.

9. F. Askeberg (1944), 97.

10. P. Buchholz (1977), 7 ff.

11. See below, and conclusion of this chapter, especially the re-(?) distribution of motifs within the *ÞS*.

12. H. Falk (1924), 25, G. Turville-Petre (1964), 61; 201.

13. J. de Vries (1957), I, 90.

14. The best discussions of these monuments are to be found in E. Ploss (1966),79 ff., *et passim.* and in H. Schück (1933), 1,172 ff.

15. The dragon-slaying is also depicted here. This sculpture was probably executed by stone masons from Scandinavia. See E. Ploss (1966), 110.

16. See Chapter IV and Chapter VII.

17. J. de Vries (1957), I, 88-89., H. Kuhn (1950), 30 ff.

18. H. de Boor believes that they were always fundamentally connected. See H. de Boor (1939), 250 ff.

19. See above regarding plastic representations.

20. The Latin alphabet did not come into widespread use in Scandinavia until the 12th-century, and our texts do not date before the 13th-century. Also there is evidence for a highly developed state of the art of public speaking in the north. Cf. M. Schlauch (1969).

21. These factors are carefully studied by P. Buchholz (1977), and T. M. Andersson (1958), 140-168.

22. P. Buchholz (1977),9 ff.

23. Cf. J. de Vries (1957), II, 154 ff; 158 ff., for a discussion of the textual history of the *CR*.

24. See Chapter IV.

25. R. Harris (1971), 347-348. Most scholars are not so kind in their judgments concerning the artistic quality of the Grp. Cf. J. de Vries (1957), II, 154 ff.

26. R. Harris (1971), 345.

27. These questions are especially interesting in light of the problems concerning the dating of the *VS* and its relationship to the *CR*.

28. J. de Vries (1956), I, 296-298.

29. A. Heusler (1919), 164 ff.

30. A. Heusler (1919), 190 ff.

31. S. Gutenbruner (1937), 135 ff.

32. J. de Vries (1956), I, 298.

33. H. Kuhn (1950), 46. Here, Kuhn follows the thoughts of F. Askeberg.

34. See Chapter VII for the importance of this motif in Germanic mythology.

35. Wieselgren 1, II, 250; III, 241. He shows that chapter 23 of the *VS* is directly borrowed from chapter 185 of the *ÞS*.

36. J. de Vries (1957), II, 469 ff.

37. R. Finch (1965), xxxvii-xxxviii. The interpolation from the *ÞS* is clearly independent, and in fact constitutes a sharp break in the continuity of the saga. The second interpolation is generally more significant to the study of the *VS*. The *VS* serves as an introduction to *Ragnars saga loðbrókar*, and it is through Áslaug, the daughter of Sigurðr and Sigrdrífa/Brynhildr that the link is made. It is unknown whether or not the character of Áslaug was invented for this purpose or whether she took on this function at a later date. In any case the connection of the *VS* with the *Ragnars saga* is probably an artificial one.

38. R. Finch (1965), xxxvii.

29. J. de Vries (1957), II, 470.

40. R. Finch (1965), xxxviii. Cf. Sd. 11 and Fm. 3; 18.

42. J. de Vries (1957), II, 471.

42. D. A. Seip (1951), 3 ff.

43. S. Einarsson (1957), 116. According to Sigudur Nordal.

44. J. de Vries (1957), II, 215-217. For a complete review of the various MSS, cf. R. C. Boer, *AaNo* (1924), 145-172.

45. *ESS* ch. 41 (*Skáldskaparmál*). See also chapter VIII.

46. J. de Vries (1957), II, 478.

47. K. Schier (1970),78; 86. As well as AM 62 fol., and GkS 2845,4° (a MS from the first fourth of the 15th-century).

48. J. de Vries (1957), II, 477.

49. Cf. *Nþ*, 317.

50. In the *VS* Óðinn departs before the battle.

51. This legend tells of Meleagros, the son of Oeneus and Althea, about whom it was foretold by the Fates upon his birth, that his life would last no longer than a torch then burning upon the hearth. His mother put the fire out and preserved the wood of the torch. Norna-Gestr was visited by *nornir* upon is birth, and was given a similar prophecy by them which involved a burning candle.

52. J. de Vries (1957), II, 477-478.

53. L. M. Hollander (1916), 106-108.

54.   E. M. Smith-Dampier (1934), 23; 30.

55.   See chapter IV.

56.   A vague reference also may remain to the cutting of the wool-flock in the stream. Cf. J. de Vries, *Studien over Færösche Balladen* (Haarlem: H. D. Tjeenk Willink & Zoon, 1915).

57.   E. M. Smith-Dampier (1934), 20. This does not, however, seem to be the case when one examines the strong correspondences between the Faeroese ballad and the Icelandic sources, and when one compares them to the relatively weak correspondences with the *ÞS* or with the *NL*.

58.   K. Schier (1970), 82-83.

59.   H. Hempel (1952), 151 ff. Hempel tries to show that the *ÞS* material was given its present form in 13th-century Saxony, and he does not see a Norse saga, but rather a Saxon chronicle (which was probably compiled between 1210 and 1230) in the form of the *ÞS*.

60.   These problems are discussed by H. Hempel (1924), 417 ff. and H. de Boor (1923), 81 ff.

61.   H. de Boor in fact does believe that Mb. closely represents the original redaction of the material. .

62.   The *ÞS* and the *NL* may be said to form the pillars of a southern tradition for the legend of Sigurðr, although they diverge widely from one another. (See ch. IV concerning the paradigmatic contrasts between the *CR-VS* version and that of the *ÞS*.

63.   J. de Vries (1961), 436-437.

64.   A. Johannesson (1951-56), 539; N. Lukman (1976), 31.

65.   J. de Vries (1961), 387.

66.   For a more exacting analysis of the problems in question here, cf. P. Buchholz (1977), esp. 124 ff.

CHAPTER FOUR

SCHEMATIZATION OF SIGURÐR'S BOYHOOD "RITES OF TRANSFORMATION"

Underlying all the sagas and lays of Young-Sigurðr is a basic three-fold structure. All the versions follow a pattern: 1) fosterage/adoption, 2) dragon-slaying, 3) meeting with Brynhildr/Sigrdrífa. However, the aim of the present thesis is only to deal with the difficult initial element of this paradigm. It is in this phase of Young-Sigurðr's heroic career that the crux of the two variant traditions first becomes important. In order to proceed in the interpretive process, the version with the most internal integrity, cultural authority, and mythological authenticity must be selected according to some criteria and then schematized to facilitate a more exhaustive interpretation in Chapter VIII.

The northern variant of the tradition presents us with a version which most completely fulfills the three requirements outlined above, although it is not without some internal variations. This northern tradition consists of the first five of the six texts commented upon in the previous chapter. Only the *ÞS* presents a structure fundamentally at variance with the generally consistent structure of the other five works. Internal structural integrity is a strong argument for ascribing the *Codex Regius*, *Völsungasaga*, *Edda Snorra Sturlusonar*, *Nornagests þáttr*, and the Faeroese *Regin smiður* to a common tradition. *Þiðrekssaga* is the only text in which Sigmundr survives past the birth of his son Sigurðr, while the mother of the hero dies upon the birth of her son. Besides the structural unity inherent in these texts, something which establishes them as belonging to a common tradition, there is also a certain stamp of cultural authority which they bear. Although the works in question arose between a wide range of dates, from ca. 900 to ca. 1350, they all portray events in the spirit of the *fornöld*. This is most interesting in contrast to the southern versions, such as the *Nibelungenlied* (ca. 1200) which is totally enmeshed in the chivalric-Christian culture. The *Þiðrekssaga* also suffers under a similar flaw from a mythological point of view, because its approach and style are so "novelistic," mundane and contemporary when compared to the saga-like quality, metaphysical occurrences and the general *in illo tempore* atmosphere portrayed in the works of the northern branch of the tradition.

Within the northern body of literature the *Völsungasaga*, supplemented by the corresponding Eddic lays, stands out as the most reliable and complete source for a study in mythology and comparative religion. The saga-writer of the *Völsungasaga* had at his disposal a body of written material, both poetic and prosaic, and he probably also had some access to contemporary oral tradition. With this corpus of information he seems to have constructed a narrative upon the firm framework provided by the earlier oral and written traditions.(1) The only possible late addition to the section of the *Völsungasaga* in question which the saga-writer could have made is the insertion of the prophecy of Sigurðr's uncle Grípir. Even this is not pure invention, but rather it is a paraphrase of the events connected with the late Eddic lay "Grípísspá." It should also be noted that the role of prophecy in the career of a hero is often an important one.(2) Thus it is possible that even this apparent interpolation could have been conceived of as an essential element in a heroic career by the saga-writer and/or by the religio-cultural milieu which the saga tries to portray.

Now, it is necessary to lay the groundwork for the body of this thesis by schematizing this section of Young-Sigurðr's career so that the various rites of transformation pertinent to the rebirth theme may be more easily discerned and subsequently interpreted with regard to the principles suggested in Chapter I. The following passage is a description of the events during this phase of Young-Sigurðr's life, with no attempt at interpretation. The structure and content of this schematic description follows that of the northern *CR-VS* (chs. 12-17) tradition quite closely, and it is this scheme which will be used in the interpretive process in Chapter VIII.

Sigmundr, the son of Völsung, along with King Eylimi goes into a battle against the sons of King Hunding in a dispute over marriage rights to Hjördís, the last wife of King Sigmundr and daughter of Eylimi. Sigmundr fights against overwhelming odds, and in the midst of the battle the figure of Óðinn enters the scene, and with his spear he breaks Sigmundr's sword, which was originally given to Sigmundr by Óðinn himself. From this moment on the tide turns against Sigmundr (... *váru Sigmundi konungi horfin heill* [*VS*. ch. 11], "good fortune was turned from Sigmundr the king"), and he is mortally wounded. After the battle, Hjördís comes to the field and finds the dying Sigmundr.(3) He tells her that she is carrying his son, and at the same time he prophesies that this boy is to be named

36

Sigurðr, whose name will endure as long as the world exists. Sigmundr entrusts the two pieces of his sword to Hjördís' care and tells her that with a sword called Gramr, which will be forged from the fragments, Sigurðr will work many great deeds, including avenging the deaths of Eylimi and Sigmundr upon the sons of Hundingr. Sigmundr dies at the dawning of the next day.(4)

Hjördís is then taken to the court of King Hjálprekr, and there she gives birth to a boy, who is immediately taken to the king. Hjálprekr recognizes the qualities of the infant when he observes the sharp eyes (in hvössu augu) of the child. The boy was then sprinkled with water and given the name "Sigurðr" (. . . vatni ausinn með Sigurðar nafni [VS. ch. 13]) by King Hjálprekr. Afterward Hjördís is married to King Álfr, son of Hjálprekr.

Sigurðr is given in fosterage(5) to the wizard-dwarf Reginn,(6) who begins to educate the young hero in a variety of kingly arts. These skills include playing chess (tafl),(7) runic lore,(8) and the speaking of many languages.(9) Reginn's tale concerning Andvari's gold hoard probably belongs to this body of teaching, however, the communication of this vital information is delayed until after Sigurðr has obtained Grani.(10)

The tutelary dwarf then urges Sigurðr to request a horse from King Hjálprekr, so that he will not appear to be a "hlaupari" (land-loper). After the king grants his request, Sigurðr starts out through the woods to choose his steed. On the way he meets einum gömlum ⁻með síðu skeggi. Sá var honum ókunnigr (an old man [= Óðinn] with a long beard. He was unknown to him) [VS. ch. 13] who asks him where he is going. Sigurðr answers: Hest skyldum vér kjósa; rað um með oss! (I am about to choose a horse; advise me on this [matter]!) [VS. ch. 13]. Óðinn then leads Sigurðr to the river Busiltjorn, where they drive all the horses into the water. All but one of the horses swim back to land, and by this method Sigurðr is able to choose his remarkable steed. The Skeggmaðrinn (bearded man) then informs Sigurðr that this horse is descended from Sleipnir, and thereupon he instructs Sigurðr to rear the horse carefully, "because he will become better than every other horse" (því at hann verðr hverjum hesti betri [VS. ch. 13]). At this point Óðinn disappears. Sigurðr then names the horse "Grani."(11)

Now Reginn tells Sigurðr the history of Andvari's hoard, which is consistently represented in the CR, VS, and the ESS.(12) While wandering through the world a divine triad consisting of Óðinn,

Loki, and Hœnir came upon Andvari's waterfall, where Loki sees an otter laying on the bank eating a salmon. Loki then throws a rock, killing the otter with one blow. Afterward the trio arrive, with the skin of the otter, at the house of Hreiðmarr. Whereupon they learn that the otter was actually Otr, the son of Hreiðmarr, and brother of Reginn and Fáfnir. Hreiðmarr demands an amount of gold sufficient to fill and cover the skin of the otter. Loki is then sent to collect the compensation. He obtains Ran's fishing net and with it he captures the dwarf Andvari, who was in the shape of a pike. In order to gain his freedom Andvari must deliver his hoard of gold into Loki's hands. This is done except for one golden ring which Andvari attempts to withhold, but Loki sees the ring and demands it also. The dwarf then places a curse upon the ring, and the hoard in general, which provides for the death of whomsoever may own the gold in the future. Loki then returns to Hreiðmarr's house where the otter-skin is first filled then covered with the gold. But Hreiðmarr notices one whisker of the otter which has been left uncovered. Óðinn is required to take the ring of Andvari, which he had also tried to retain, and with it, cover the whisker. After the gods depart, Fáfnir kills his father and takes the gold. In order to better guard the hoard, Fáfnir transforms himself into a lindworm, or serpent. Reginn relates this tale to Sigurðr to convince him to slay Fáfnir and win the gold for himself.

In order to perform this great deed Sigurðr must have a powerful weapon. Therefore Sigurðr requests that Reginn forge a great sword by means of his skill.(13) The smith tries on two occasions to forge the weapon, but both times it fails Sigurðr's stern anvil-test, which consists of striking Reginn's anvil with the blade of the sword.(14) After these failures Sigurðr goes to his mother, Hjördís, and after taking drink with her, asks: *Hvárt höfum vér rétt til spurt, at Sigmundr konungr seldi yðr sverðit Gram í tveim hlutum?* (Whether I have heard correctly that Sigmundr the king gave you the sword Gramr in two pieces?) [*VS* ch. 15]).(15) Hjördís delivers the shards to him, whereupon Sigurðr returns to Reginn and requests that the smith reforge the sword. When Reginn emerges from the smithy with the blade— *sýndist smiðjusveinum sem eldar brynni ór eggjunum*— "It seemed to the apprentices as if fire were burning from the edges" [*VS* ch. 15]. Sigurðr strikes the anvil with the sword, and the anvil is split down into the stock.(16) Then Sigurðr takes a mass of wool and places it in a river,(17) upstream, and as it comes toward him, he places Gramr in the water and allows the wool to drift against the blade, and instantly the wool is split in two.(18)

At this point in the VS(19) Sigurðr goes to to his *móðirbróðir* Grípir who foretells the *ørlög* of the hero, but only after Sigurðr's vehement request to hear the *spá*, or prophesy. The Eddic lay Grípisspá.(20) is a collective vision of the entirety of the *Niflungasaga* from this point to the tragedy of Guðrún. However, for purposes of this study, only the initial ten stanzas are of importance. In the ninth stanza Grípir prophesies that Sigurðr will avenge his father and Eylimi by killing the sons of Hundingr:

> *Fyrst muntu, fylkir,*   *fǫður um hefna*
> *oc Eylima*   *allz harms reca;*
> *þú munt harða*   *Hundings sono,*
> *snialla, fella,*   *mundu sigr hafa.*

(First, o chieftain, you will avenge your father and Eylimi — avenge all the sorrow — you will kill the hardy sons of Hunding, those brave ones, [and] you will have victory.)

[Grp. 9]

The avenging of Sigmundr by his son Sigurðr is an important element in all five versions found in the northern textual tradition. Siguðr approaches King Hjáprekr with a request for an army and equipment for a war of revenge on the sons of Hundingr, and his requirements are copiously met by the king. The army sets out across the sea in an armada of long-ships, however, a few days into the journey a storm breaks and the ships are tossed in rough water. A man suddenly appears and requests to be taken aboard Sigurðr's ship. When they ask his name, he replies:

> *Hnicar*(21) *héto mic,*   *þá er Hugin gladdi*
> *Vǫlsungr ungi*   *oc vegit hafði.*
> *Nú máttu kalla*   *karl af bergi,*
> *Feng eða Fiǫlni;*(21)   *far vil ec þiggia.*(22)

(They call me Hnikkar   when Huginn was gladdened
the young Völsungr   also had been killed.
Now you may call [me]   the man of the mountain,
Fengr or Fjölnir;   I want to get aboard.)

[Rm. 18]

39

When he cones aboard the storm ceases. The hero then addresses Hnikkar and requests that he impart war-wisdom. Whereupon Hnikkar speaks some didactic verses, which are related in both the *CR* and in the *Nþ*.(23) Here Óðinn instructs Sigurðr in the arts of divination by omen, in war tactics, including the use of the phalanx, and in the ethics and wisdom of the warrior.(24) When the ship reaches the land of the sons of Hundingr, Hnikkar disappears. Following his curious incident Sigurðr carries out the mass slaughter of Hundingr's sons and their army, all of whom are no match for the hero and his invincible sword, Gramr. After completing his deed of vengeance with the *blóðörn*,(25) Sigurðr returns ot the land of Hjálprekr ". . . *með fögrum sigri ok miklu fé ok ágæti* (with fair victory and great and excellent wealth) [VS ch. 17]. There great feasts are made for him in celebration of his victory.

Now that the main elements of the initial phase of the Sigurðr's story have been described, they should be schematized in order to make the sequence of stages clear and at the same time provide a convenient method of analyzing the stages for future interpretation. This analysis is intended to place the motifs present in the *Sigurðarsaga* into a framework of stages (*Stationen*) expressed in the *CR-VS* version of the myth. Each of these stages is composed of either a motif, or a complex of motifs which may be functionally assimilated for purposes of this analysis. The staged sequence does not necessarily represent a universal Germanic paradigm, although there are many correspondences in other Germanic documents.(26) The sequence seems to be governed by certain internal paradigmatic "laws"(27) which at least appear to be characteristic of this version of the Sigurðr myth. The initial situation portrays the motif of the posthumous son. The concept of the father being reborn in a posthumous son should be initially understood and interpreted separately from the subsequent *Stationen des Heldenlebens*. This is because it cannot be considered a common stage within the initiatory paradigm, but in the case of the *Sigurðarsaga* it is an integral part of the mythic paradigm of the "initiation" of the exemplary model. This initial situation is followed by a sequence of events leading up to the avenging of the dead father. The son undergoes the ritual of *vatni ausa*, and is thereafter fostered to a semi-hostile *úmannligr* figure. There is then a period of education in numerous areas of knowledge, in which the hero learns wisdom, kingly arts, ancient lore, and military tactics. The didactic verses spoken by Hnikarr could be functionally included in this stage. The reception of the most important insignia of the warrior-king, the horse and the sword (weapon), forms a two-fold stage of central importance. The prophecy of Grípir could possibly be included in the education stage, however, because of its possible magical implications and synthesizing(55) function it should perhaps appear in its natural position. While the final stage is the avenging of the father by the son, who is the father reborn. A convenient scheme of this paradigm would appear:

      0. Posthumous son
      I. *Vatni ausa*
      II. Fosterage
      III. Education
      IV. Gifts
           A. Horse (Grani)
           B. Sword (Gramr)
      V. Prophecy
      VI. Vengeance

For the northern branch of the *Sigurðarsaga the thematic paradigm would appear:

      I.   Father killed
      II. A. Mother protects son (father reborn)
           B. Son prepared for revenge (with father's weapon)
      III. Son avenges father

This pattern provides a clear contrast to a similar scheme erected for the *Þiðrekssaga af Bern* paralleling this phase of Sigurðr's life:

      I.   Mother dies — child lost
      II. A. Child nurtured by beasts
           B. Child fostered by smith
      III. Child attains monstrous strength

From this method of comparison it is possible to determine that at this parallel point in the two sagas, we are dealing with two fundamentally different motifs: one "the avenging son," and the other, "the heroic waif." It is not the purpose of this work to determine which of the two motifs is "older" or the "original version" ' of the legend of Sigurðr. However, according to the three criteria set down at the outset of this chapter, the northern version presents the most internally integral, culturally authoritative. and mythologically authentic, For this reason the northern branch provides the most promising material for an interpretation of the type offered in this work.

Footnotes to Chapter Four

1. See chapter III.
2. See chapter VII.
3. Here there is a striking parallel between the *Völsungasaga* and the Faeroese *Regin smiður*. In the Faeroese *kvæði* we find:

11. *Hoyr tú reysti Sigmundur,*	Hear, brave Sigmundur
søti min,	my sweet,
eru tey nakað grøðandi	are there any herbs
sárini tín?	for your wounds?
12. *Seint mannst tú Hjørdis,*	You may be too late, Hjørdis,
fáa til tess ráð	to do anything about it
gera tey smyrslini,	to make those ointments,
sum grøða míni sár.	which will heal my wound.

While in the *Völsungasaga* in the parallel position there see: (*Hjördís spyrr:*) . . . *ef hann væri græðandi; en hann svarar: "Margr lifnar or lítlum vánum, en horfin eru mér heill, svá at ek vil [eigi] láta græða mik* . . . [VS ch. 12]. (Hjördís asks:) if he might be able to be healed; but he answers: "Many [men] become healthy from little hope; but good fortune has turned from me, so that I do not want to have myself healed ..."

This is especially remarkable when we consider the relative obscurity of this motif within the overall structure and the probable textual history of the Faeroese *kvæði*. See chapter III.

4. In all the versions of the northern tradition the circumstances surrounding the death of Sigmundr are almost identical. Although the *CR* contains no particular lay relating Sigmundr's death, the latter half of the Rm. presupposes the event in the same form found elsewhere.

5. On the matter of Sigurðr's fosterage in the northern tradition, only the Faeroese *Regin smiður* diverges from the version presented here. In this *kvæði* we read:

41. *Hann vaks upp í ríkinum*	He grew up in the kingdom
til geviligan mann,	to [be] a lucky man,
Hjálprek kongurin	Hjálprek the king
fostraði hann.	fostered him.

See also chapter III and chapter VI for the general importance of fosterage.

6. The *ætt*, or race of beings, to which Reginn belongs is somewhat in question, however, it is certain that he did not originally belong to the *mannaætt*, that is, he was not a human being. Various textual passages attest to this assumption. When describing Reginn, both the *CR* and the *Nþ.* use similar phrases: "*dvergr of vǫxt*" (the prose at the beginning of the "Reginsmál"), and "*dvergr á vöxt*" (Nþ. chs. 4; 5) . However, Reginn refers to his own brother, Fáfnir, in terms of the *jötnaætt* in "Fáfnismál" 29.3, when he refers to the dead sibling as "*inn aldna jǫtun.*" It can be assumed that this circumstance would also assign Reginn to the

43

jötnaætt, or at least to some *úmannlig ætt*. This supposition is strengthened by two other occurrences in the *Elder Edda*. Reginn is said to drink the venomous blood of his slain brother, an act which would usually be fatal to normal humans, but in Reginn's case it renders a positive magical effect (see chapter VIII). Also the name "Reginn" appears in the "Dvergatal" in the Vsp. 12.7. It is not certain that these two figures are identical. The *VS* never refers to Reginn in terms of the *dverga-* or *jötnaætt*, and the word "*maðr*" is often used when describing him as well. These last two points are best ascribed to a later tradition, as it is most probable that Reginn originally belonged to an *úmannlig ¯ætt*, but with the passage of time lost this attribution. As to the use of the term "wizard" in describing Reginn, evidence in this direction is universal within the northern branch. Both the *CR* (first prose section in "Reginsmál") and *Nþ*. ch. 4 use the adjective "*fjölkunnigr*" when describing him. While the *Völsungasaga* tells of him teaching Sigurðr runic lore (which could be either magical or didactic, but it is most likely merely the skill of reading and writing in runic characters) [VS ch. 13]. The *ESS* describes Hreiðmarr, the father of Reginn, with the phrase "*mioc fiolkvNigr*" [*ESS* 47 (39), 127:8]. In the Faeroese *Regin smiður* it is quite apparent that the process of reforging the sword, Gramm, is to a great extent a magical one, involving a 3 x 3 formula. Three times Regin attempts the work, each time with a three-fold process:

88.	*Regin gongur at smiðinum,*	Regin goes to the smithy
	legði svørð í eld	laid the sword into the fire
	tríati næturnar	for three nights
	hevði hann tað í gerð.	he had that in construction.

The process contained in this stanza is repeated twice more before the reforging is completed successfully. The possible implications of the name "Reginn" will be discussed below in chapter VIII, see also chapter III above.

7. Chess as we commonly know it today is of course not an indigenous Germanic feature, however, the game originally indicated may very well have been *hnefatafl*, see C. Tolkien (1960) 88-89, an apparently indigenous Scandinavian "hunt-game," as opposed to a "war-game," which is how chess would be classified. See chapter VII for the possible significance of this game.

8. The runic lore imparted here could be that which is the privilege of the *dvergaætt*; cf. Háv. 144.3, which indicates that there are runes (*arcana*) for each classification of beings: "*Dvalinn dvergom fyrir.*" See chapter VII.

9. These languages may be those of mankind (Germanic dialects, etc.), but they may also be the languages of the various *ættir* as described throughout the didactic "Alvíssmál." Here, the dwarf Alvíss relates the names for things as they are called in the various worlds: "*heimi hveriom í*", e.g., in Miðgarðr, in Ásgarðr, in Jötunheimr, in Álfheimr. See chapter VII.

10. This sequence holds for both the *VS* and the Rm.

11. Only the *VS* transmits all these details concerning the choosing of Grani. In the *CR* the prose beginning the Rm. states simply "*Sigurðr gecc til stóðs Hjálprecs oc kaus sér af hest einn, er Grani var kallaðr síðan*" (Sigurðr went to Hjálprekr's stud farm and chose a horse for himself, which was called Grani

afterward). The *Edda* of Snorri first mentions Grani at the time when Sigurðr removes the gold from Fáfnir's lair, while the *Nþ.* neglects to mention the horse at all. In the Faeroese *Regin smíður* we find a variant form for the method the hero employs in order to choose his steed, and it is not Óðinn, but his mother Hjørdis, who instructs him concerning the special procedure he is to follow:

63. *Hann gekk Sær at fossinum*
    kastaði stein í á,
    tók sær tann av hestunum
    sum ikki víkti frá.

(He went to the stream, threw a stone into the river, took for himself that one of the horses which did not flinch from [the stone]).

This contains some of the same elements found in the *VS*: instruction from an advisor and procedure connected to a river. While a test of the horse's courage in water is at the root of both methods.

12. In the Rm. (first prose section and sts. 1-12), *VS* chapter 14, and the *ESS* chapters 47(30) and 48. The myth of the *otrgjöld* is probably of great antiquity, whether or not it was originally connected to the *Sigurðarsaga. See chapter III concerning the Rm.

13. All versions in the northern tradition generally represent the actual forging of Gramr in the same manner.

14. In the Faeroese "Regin smiður" Sjúrður owns the shards of Sigmundr's sword from the beginning of the forging process, and therefore it is the art of the smith and not the material with which he is working that facilitates the reforging of Gramr. See Note 6 in this chapter. This constitutes the most divergent variant within the northern branch.

15. Only the *VS* and "Regin smiður" describe Sigurðr receiving the shards of Gramr from his mother. The other versions simply state that Reginn forged the sword for him. "Regin smiður" provides an interesting parallel of the reception of the shards. Hjørdis says to Sjúrður:

57. *Tak tu hesar*   Take   these
    svøroslutir tvá   two sword pieces
    lat tu tær eitt annað   have   another sword
    svørðið av teim slá.   forged for yourself from them.

Here the insistence on two pieces is important in both versions. In the Faeroese *kvæði* Sjúrður also receives the blood stained byrnie which belonged to Sigmundur (st. 55).

16. This anvil-test motif is presented in all five versions found within the northern tradition.

17. The river is identified as the "Rín" (Rhine) in the *CR* (prose after st. 14) and in *Nþ.* ch. 5.

18. The motif of the wool-in-the-stream test appears in all the versions except the Faeroese "Regin smiður."

19. The position of the prophecy of Grípir in the *VS* is roughly determined by the contents of the Grp., which the saga-writer probably knew. This Eddic lay is set in a time after Sigurðr has obtained Grani (and probably after Gramr has been forged, as it is not mentioned in the prophecy) and just before he sets out to avenge Sigmundr.

20. See chapter III.

21. Óðinn. These names of Óðinn are also found in the "Grímnismál" 47.3; 5.

22. This st. also appears in the *VS*.

23. These stanzas are found in the Rm. 18-25, and in *Nþ*. ch. 6.

24. For a discussion of the functional importance of these verses, and of their content, see chapter VIII.

25. The ritual of "carving the blood-eagle" is related in the *CR* (Rm. 26), and in the *Nþ*. ch. 6.

26. See chapter VI.

27. The importance of the sequence of stages is discussed in chapter VII.

CHAPTER FIVE

NORSE CONCEPTIONS OF THE SOUL
AND THE IDEOLOGIES OF *APTRBURÐR*
AND DIVINE PROGENITORSHIP

Research concerning the study of the soul,(1) and its many functions, and the ideology of rebirth as conceptualized by the old Germanic peoples, has had a varied history, as evidenced in Chapter II of this work. The general ideas central to the belief in souls and rebirth have claimed some attention in almost all the major handbooks(2) dealing with the history of ancient Germanic religion. Valuable studies have been contributed to this field by V. Grönbech, ¯M. Keil, K. Eckhardt, J. de Vries, and most recently, by H. R. E. Davidson and E. Mundal.(3) This chapter outlines the general northern Germanic beliefs concerning the soul and the various entities which constitute the soul, insofar as they are important to the formulation of the doctrines of rebirth and divine progenitorship among the northern Germanic peoples. It is not, however, intended that this chapter should serve as a comprehensive treatment of the vast Germanic *Seelenvorstellungen*. The various soul-entities will be touched upon in order to provide a matrix of perspective for the concepts central to the present argument. For the most part, it is the *hamingja-flygja* complex, that which is usually thought to be transferred from generation to generation, which concerns us here. An attempt will be made to demonstrate the Germanic belief in the rebirth (ON *aftrburðr* or *endburðr*) of the "soul" (ON *hamingja*, *flygja, et al.*), and to show the origin of this soul among the gods—at least in the case of the Völsungar.

Old Norse is rich in words indicative of a set of qualities and/or entities which are attached to an individual, but which are in varying degrees distinct from the physical body. In most cases, attempts to find one-word English definitions or translations(4) for these words will fall far short of their goal. Many terms such as ON *önd*: "breath, the breath of life" and ON *óðr*: "inspired mental activity",(5) have often been thought to indicate members of this set of soul-concepts. However, the nature of these terms is actually quite different from the type which we are discussing here. *Önd* and *óðr*, along with several other words, denote activities, qualities, forces, or essences which are active within a man's psychosomatic complex, but which

47

do not approach the measure of autonomy or transferable characteristics which are central to concepts examined here. There is, therefore, a substantial distinction between the qualities of these terms and the qualities of another, more autonomous, and in most instances personifiable, set of concepts. This latter group of terms gives us more opportunity to gain a metaphysical background for the understanding of the Germanic rebirth doctrine.

Within this set of semi-autonomous concepts we may discern four major entities or functions—the *hugr*, the *hamr*, the *hamingja*, and the *flygja*. These should probably be best understood as interlocking aspects of the same all-encompassing concept, which for purposes of this study, will be called "soul."

Hugr

The *hugr* is variously defined in terms of modern English concepts as "mind," "thought," "heart," "mood," "desire," or "courage."(6) "Awareness" may also be inferred from this set of concepts.(7) However, the *hugr* is often described in such a way that it displays affinities with the other three concepts in question. The *hugr* is sometimes said to appear in animal shape, but this usually takes place in the world of dream. *Harðar saga ok Hólmverja* tells of a woman who dreams that eighty wolves came to her house. These wolves are interpreted to be the "foreboding" *hugir* of the Hólmverjar.(8) Of the terms discussed here, the *hugr* is the least often personified. It may be projected from the body to perform various tasks, such as fetching home a horse from the field, or doing mischief.(9) The etymology. of the term *"hugr"* is a difficult problem, and no completely satisfactory solution has been offered. It does, however, appear in all the major Germanic dialects,(10) and is therefore probably an extremely old concept, and one belonging to the oldest set of common Germanic ideas. The *hugr* is called the *"trollkvenna vindr"* because it is connected with the force of air which may be projected from the lungs. The stronger the force of expelled air, the more powerful the *hugr* is said to be.(11) Perhaps the most important trait of the *hugr* is its role as a tutelary genius. In this aspect it finds a unique place in the structure of the Germanic soul. To be in complete communication with it is a sign of *heill hugr* (whole mind), a high level of consciousness, and this will reward a man with good *ráð*.(12) Only then may a man speak with sincerity. It is apparent that the *hugr* is the cognitive element, which is an integral part of the individual's soul, and which can also be projected forth from the individual to travel alone, or in conjunction with other aspects of the psychosomatic complex.(13)

Hamr

The *hamr* seems to stand at an opposite pole in relation to the *hugr*, within the paradigm implied by the four terms discussed here. It is also apparent that a powerful *hugr* can have control over the *hamr*. This term may be defined roughly as either "skin" or "shape."(14) This "shape" is the semi-plastic image creating essence which can be molded by the *hugr* into forms of various types, e.g., animals. The phenomenon of *hamrammr* was originally that of transforming the human hamr into that resembling an animal. In certain initiatory practices the initiate may don an animal skin in order to symbolize the psycho-physical transformation which is to take place as a result of this magical operation.(15) This is illustrated by the story of Sigmundr and Sinfjötli in the *VS* ch. 8. This is, in the final analysis, not a case of the human will (*hugr*) assuming the animation of a previously existing animal form (*hamr*). Rather, it is the creation of a new *hamr*, by the *hugr* out of its own essence.(16) When this phenomenon takes place, the person's normal body loses all signs of animate life, as the *hamr* departs and is reshaped elsewhere.(17) The *hugr* must already contain the essence peculiar to the entity into which it transforms itself, and furthermore, the quality of this essence is always present in the body.(18) These shapes (*hamir*), which *seiðmenn* and *seiðkonur* may create with the power of their *hugir*, have a strong link with their own "physical" bodies. If a *hamr* is injured in a fight, the body of the person who sent the shape will manifest the wounds as well. A *hamr* may also be killed.(19) This belief was common and continued into modern times.(20)

A *hamr* is also identified with the afterbirth, "the skin in which the fruit is enclosed." In Germany when a child was born enveloped within the afterbirth, it was termed a *Glückshaube*, and was considered a good omen. The afterbirth was thought to contain a soul-like essence which would follow the child as a guardian spirit.(21) Therefore the afterbirth would be stored away, or sewn into a band and placed around the child's body.(22) Here, the roots of the concepts *hamingja* and *fylgja* are first made apparent.

We now come to the terms which are at the crux of the question in this thesis: the *hamingja* and the *fylgja*. Both of these entities are

49

closely bound together and in turn this complex is firmly woven into the overall structural fabric of the soul. However, it is these aspects, with all the qualities inherent in them, which may be transferred from one person to another, and as such lie at the heart of the technical, metaphysical theory of rebirth among the northern Germanic peoples.

Hamingja

This term carries with it a three-pronged definition, all stemming from the basic concept "*hamr.*" The first definition is that of "the shape-changing force." This is derived from the "soul-form" or "image" aspect of the *hamr*, as outlined above. It is the power which acts upon the *hamr* in order to effect transformations. The second definition is the more common "luck" or "fortune." There are a variety of Old Norse terms for "luck," such as *gipta*, *gæfa*, or *heill*, but these are not central to this argument.(23) The third meaning could simply be "guardian spirit." The latter two are also derived from an aspect of the *hamr*, that of the *Glückshaube*, which was a sign of luck, magical force, and the guardian spirit.(24) Thus from two aspects of a single term we have two distinct functions, which were probably syncretically understood by the ancient Northmen. The concepts "soul" and "luck" are also similarly understood by peoples of other cultures. Holmberg reports, concerning the Finns, that they have two words, *haltia*: "a soul-like essence which aids man," and *onni*: "luck," which are two words for the same basic concept.(25) The *hamingja* is the "indwelling luck," which is embodied in a (protective) spiritual being. This force is essentially dynamistic,(26) however, it is often anthropomorphized in some literary accounts. The common Old Norse expression: *leggja sina hamingju með einhverjum*,(27) is very instructive in the former regard, while the anthropomorphic description given in *Víga-Glums saga* ch. 9 is interesting in light of the latter tendency, although we might expect the term *fylgja* in this context. The passage from *Víga-Glums saga* reads:

> *Þat er sagt, at Glúm dreymði eina nótt. Hann þóttist vera úti staddr á bæ sínum ok sjá út til fjarðarins. Hann þóttist sjá konu eina ganga útan eftir heraðinu, ok stefndi þangat til Þverár, en hon var svá mikil, at axlirnar tóku ut fjöllin tveggja vegna. En hann þóttist ganga ór garði*

*á móti henni ok bauð henni til sín, ok síðan vaknaði
hann. Öllum þótti undarligt, en hann segir svá: "Draumr
er mikill ok merkiligr, en svá mun ek hann raða, at
Vígfuss, móðirfaðir minn, mun nú vera andaðr, ok mundi
kona sjá hans hamingja vera, er fjöllum hæra gekk. Ok
var hann um aðra menn fram um flesta hluti at virðingu,
ok hans hamingja mun leita sér þangat staðfestu, sem ek
em.*(28)

(It is said, that Glúmr dreamed one night. He seemed to
be standing outside on his farm and looking out toward
the fjord. He seemed to see a woman come from there
through the open country, and went toward Þvera, and
she was so huge, that her shoulders touched the
mountains on two sides. And he thought he went from
the enclosure toward her and bid her to him, and then he
woke up. It seemed strange to everyone, but about it he
said: "The dream is great and significant, and I will
interpret it thusly, that Vígfuss, my maternal grandfather, must have just died, and the woman was probably
his *hamingja*, who walked higher than the mountains.
And he was superior to other men as regards worthiness
in most matters, and his *hamingja* will therefore seek for
herself a residence, like I am.)

Thus it is clear that it was believed that the *hamingja* could be sent
forth in part, or in its entirety, both while the "sender" was alive, or
upon his death, and by this sending he could transmit a set of
spiritual qualities to a recipient. In the case of Víga-Glúmr he
received a spear, a cloak, and a sword from Vígfuss as signs
betokening the future transfer of power—and as long as he kept these
talismans, the *hamingja* of Vígfuss was with him.(29) This "sending"
aspect is most probably the basis for the etymology of the term,
which was first forwarded by H. Falk, *hamingja* < *ham-gengja*:
either "one who lets their *hamr* go forth" or "one who goes about in
an alien *hamr*."(30) It is also evident that a man may have more than
one *hamingja*, and that, in fact it is a mark of great power to possess
many *hamingjur*.(31)

All the ramifications of the *hamingja* are too complex to enter
into here, however, from what has already been said, it is possible to

see how this powerful essence could be passed from person to person, and from generation to generation.

V. Grönbech attempts to explain the success of King Haraldr Hárfagr in terms of *hamingja*, which he gathered from various ancestors and clan members. King Hálfdan inn svarti had a son by the daughter of King Haraldr "Goldbeard." This son was given to Haraldr in fosterage and he gave him the name Haraldr. In the interim, Hálfdan had another son by a powerful woman named Ragnhildr Sigurðardóttir. The two Haraldrs died at about the same time, and subsequently the name and the *hamingja* passed to the son of Hálfdan and Ragnhildr—Haraldr Hárfagr. Thus Haraldr gathered *hamingjur* from at least four separate sources.(32) An attempt will be made to clarify this process in the sections below dealing with rebirth and the naming customs connected to this doctrine. A child is said to derive *hamingja* or luck from both the father and the mother,(33) while a foster-father may also impart a degree of *hamingja* to his *fóstri*.(34)

The *hamingja* appears to function as a bridge concept between the purely dynamistic entities such as *önd*, *óðr*, *hugr* and *hamr* and the more animistic entities such as the *fylgja* and *dísir*. Essentially, it is a dynamistic force, which can be stored up, and projected in accordance with the human will in order to effect changes in the environment but it is also the embodiment of a personal moral "law." That is, it carries obligations as well as power. The connection of the Nornir with the concept of the *hamingja*, which is made in the "Vafðruðnismál" sts. 48-49, would support this idea.(35) It is a constant entity which is supported and supplied with strength by members of the clan.(36) The *hamingja* is fed by deeds of honor; it is a cumulative quality, and can grow almost indefinitely. This emphasis on the clan in this particular context seems to almost presuppose the doctrine of *aftrburðr* within its structure.

Fylgja

With regard to the metaphysical clanic structure the concept of the *fylgja* has a special crystalizing aspect to offer, that of the *ættarfylgja*: "the *fylgja* of the clan or family." But before discussing this important concept we should first examine the basic term "*fylgja*" and make some determinations concerning its basic nature. In many respects the *fylgja* is almost identical to the *hamingja*. Both concepts were probably developed from a perception of realities within the realm of dream. The *fylgja* should be understood through that aspect of the *hamingja* known as the "guardian spirit," and as such it is understood to be a form, usually invisible, which "follows" a person. This may be in an gynomorphic (female) form or in the shape of an animal.(37) However, the *fylgja* as well as the *hamingja* must not be thought of as forms, but rather as aspects of the "spiritual" essence itself, which was originally equated with the procreative power and potency of a man. In later times the two terms were sometimes confused with one another.(38) Probably the most important distinctions between the *hamingja* and the *fylgja* is that the *fylgja* remains attached to a person until the time of death, while the *hamingja* may be, in varying degrees, projected from the individual and actually given to someone else,(39) and that the *hamingja* rarely, if ever, has negative or disadvantageous connotations. The best etymology for this term seems to be a derivation from the Old Norse verbal form *fylgja*: "to follow,"(40) therefore the "following spirit," and also the "afterbirth."

Furthermore, we might distinguish between two important sub-divisions within the common idea of the *fylgja*, i.e., the *mannsfylgja* and a *fylgja* which embodies the power of a whole clan, i.e., the *ættarfylgja* or *kynfylgja*. The *mannsfylgja* is born with the individual and it may act as a link between the person and his *ættarfylgja*.(41) The *ættarfylgja* is attached to a certain member of the clan, usually its chief, and when he dies it will choose another member of the clan, usually the chief's son, and attach itself to him.(42) This entity carries with it the good fortune, and special powers of the clan. Again, this concept is central to the special Germanic belief in rebirth, and it is this idea of an *ættarfylgja* which is most important to the present work.

There are many occurrences of the *fylgja* in Old Norse literature. In the HHj. prose after st. 30 we read that Heðinn, the brother of Helgi, meets a *trollkona* who is riding a wolf using snakes as reins. This *trollkona* asks if she might "follow" Heðinn. Later, when Helgi and Heðinn meet, after Heðinn has inadvertently sworn a solemn oath to take Sváva, Helgi's beloved *valkyrja* from him, it is said of Helgi that: "*hann grunaði um feigð sína oc þat, at fylgior hans hǫfðo vitiað Heðins, þá er hann sa kanona ríða varginom*" (... he suspected it was a sign of death and that it was his fylgjur [pl.] who had met Heðinn, when he saw the woman riding on the wolves.) [Prose following HHj. st. 34.]

53

Then he says:

35. Reið á vargi   er recqvið var,
    flióð eitt, er hann   fylgio beiddi;
    on vissi þat,   at veginn myndi
    Sigrlinnar sonr   á Sigarsvǫllom.

(A woman was riding   on a wolf
when it was twilight,   who asked to be [Heðinn's] fetch;
she knew   that Sigrlinn's son
would be killed   on Sigrar's-plain.)

In this situation it is clear that the *fylgja* knows that Helgi is doomed, and therefore wants to "follow" his brother Heðinn. The *Völsungasaga* itself contains a reference to the *ættarfylgja* of the Völsungar. In ch. 4, with reference to her marriage to Siggeirr, Signý says to Völsungr:
". . . "*veit ek af framvisi minni ok af kynfylgju várri, at af þessu ráði stendr oss mikill úfagnaðr, ef eigi er skjótt brugðit þessum ráðahag.*" (I know from my foreknowledge and from our kin-*fylgja*, that from this counsel great sorrow will fall on us, if this marriage is not broken quickly.) This passage is also indicative of the magical aspect of the *fylgja*, which in this case imparts the ability of "second-sight."

The passage in Old Norse literature which best demonstrates the special properties of the *ættarfylgja*, and illustrates some of the apparently common secondary motifs which accompany its appearance, is found in the *Hallfreðar saga*, ch. 11:

Þá sá þeir konu ganga eftir skipinu. Hon var mikil ok í brynju. Hon gekk á bylgjum sem á landi. Hallfreðr leit til ok sá, at par var fylgjukona hans. Hallfreðr mælti: "Í sundr segi ek öllu við þik." Hon mælti: "Viltu, Þorvaldr, taka við mér?" Hann kvaðst eigi vilja. Þá mælti Hallfreðr ungi: "Ek vil taka við þér." Siðan hvarf hon. Þá mælti Hallfreðr: "Þér, sonr minn, vil ek gefa sverðit konungsnaut, en aðra gripi skal leggja í kistu hjá mér, ef ek öndumst hér á skipinu.

(Then they saw a woman going behind the ship. She was great in size and was in a byrnie. She walked on the

54

waves as if on land. Hallfreðr looked [at her] and saw that she was his "fetch-woman." Hallfreðr said: "I declare everything at an end with you." She said: Þorvaldr, do you want to receive me?" He said he did not want to. Then Hallfreðr the young spoke: "I want to receive you." Then she disappeared. Then Hallfreðr said: "To you, my son, I want to give the sword 'kings-gift,' but the other treasures shall be laid in the casket beside me if I die here on the ship.)

The secondary motifs are the gift (the sword),(43) and the similarity, or identity of names. Also it is common that the appearance of the *fylgja* to its possessor is a foreboding of his death.(44) The *Hallfreðar saga* is definitely a document of the Christian period, however, it is safe to assume that in this particular instance the saga is portraying an essentially heathen motif.(45) This is not the case with some of the occurrences of the *fylgjur* in Old Norse documents. The concept of the *fylgja* seems to have been recast into a "Christian" mold at an early date. "Christian," qualified here, because of the thousand years in which the Christian doctrines, official and unofficial, had been influenced by the indigenous Indo-European beliefs which were gradually assimilated into Christian thought.(46) A prime example of this process is the case of a certain Síðu-Hallr, who, in *Njálssaga* ch. 100, states that he would like to have the archangel Michael as his *fylgju engill*.(47) Often we find that Christian influence has managed to alter the nature of belief in *fylgjur* by introducing a struggle between good and evil. In such a case a man may have a set of good *fylgjur* and a set of evil ones attached to him.(48) Although the heathen system admits multiple *fylgjur* they were not portrayed so much in terms of good and evil, but on the contrary they would present a united form with a single will.(49) Moreover, the multiplicity of *fylgjur* seems to be indicative of the relative strength of the possessor of those *fylgjur*. The more *fylgjur* a man may have, the more powerful his *ættarfylgja* may come to be.(50) These various entities would probably originate in the individuals of different branches of the clan, and through specific conditions and cultic practices these entities would devolve upon one exemplary member of the clan, and become attached to him.

The *fylgja*, which often appears as a large feminine being, is usually not the *fylgja* of the individual (*mannsfylgja*), but rather that of the clan (*ættarfylgja*) which actually represents the *"wirkende Macht der Sippe."*(51) This entity carries the authority, the responsibility, and the "higher force" which resides in the chieftain.(52) The *fylgjur* have often been associated with the *dísir*, and there is also strong evidence to suggest that the *valkyrjur* may also be related to the *fylgja* and *hamingja* concepts.(53) The most weighty arguments may be drawn from some of the oldest material in the *CR*. In the Helgi-lays, all of the "Helgar" are attached to *valkyrjur*, and they act as guardian spirits, as dispensers of gifts and wisdom, and as lovers.(54) The opening stanzas of the "Völundarkviða," in which the *valkyrjur*, Hlaðguðr svanhvit, Hervor alvítr, and Qlrún play an important role,(55) may be interpreted to mean that because Völundr did not seek his *valkyrja*, "alvítr" (all-wise), misfortune befell him.(56) Also the passage cited above from *Hallfreðar saga* shows a trace of this concept, only from a reversed perspective, that is, the *fylgja* manifests *valkyrja*-like traits, e.g., the byrnie.

Concerning this whole question of the nature of the *fylgja*, W. Golther in 1895 already summed it up quite well when he wrote: *"In den fylgjur verkörpern sich gewissermassen die eignen Seele der einzelnen Menschen und zugleich die Seelen der abgeschiedenen Ahnen, aber als selbstständige Wesen gedacht."*(57)

The description "animistic" has been applied to the concept of the *fylgja*,(58) and while this may now be a questionable use of this term, the *fylgja* is the most anthropomorphized of the various soul-entities, and one which developed what seems to be a will of its own. From the viewpoint of the individual this seems to be quite true, but viewed from the perspective of the *ætt*, another picture begins to take form. To the individual who might be unconscious of his genealogical heritage, and who has not actualized the power potentially residing in his *ættarfylgja*, the forces of "fate" seem to compel certain actions and situations. Therefore, the *fylgja* is said to have a will of its own. However, once the individual becomes conscious of the past, and integrates himself into the power (*hamingja*?) of his (*ættar-*)*fylgja* through deeds of honor or through acquisition of numinous knowledge, or through particular rites of transformation, or a combination of any of these elements, then it becomes somewhat more evident that the "being" which seems to be other than himself, is actually the sum total of all that he is, and all that he has done.(59) In some cases this set of powers and obligations may be to a certain degree imparted from a source outside the individual's direct line of genealogical descent.(60) These conclusions presuppose a particular *hamingja-(ættar-)fylgja* complex. Certain similarities between the concepts *hamingja* and *fylgja* have already been noted, and their structural connections will be discussed further in the next section of this chapter. Here, however, we are only concerned with the two concepts insofar as they are functions of causality or "fate." The stanzas from "Vafðrúðnismál" cited above indicate that the three Nornir are closely related to the *hamingja* concept, while J. de Vries points out that the *ættarfylgja* acts as a causal agent in the lives of men.(61) It seems that the all-encompassing power, potency, and obligation is contained in the *hamingja* and is embodied in the *ættarfylgja*. The *hamingja-fylgja* complex would therefore seem to be the "personal" storehouse of *ørlög*, as it is so brilliantly interpreted by P. Bauschatz, i.e., the destiny which man creates for himself through past accomplishments.(62) When this process is extended in its scope to include former existences ("lives") in which a *hamingja* and/or *ættarfylgja* was active, the ideas take on a new importance, and increased power. The autonomy, or animistic nature, which is sometimes considered a primary characteristic of the *fylgja* concept, may be reinterpreted along dynamistic lines if the arguments presented here are accepted. This apparently autonomous being is actually the incorporation of past human action, which is formulated into *ørlög* by the Nornir(63) and subsequently "spoken" by them. That is, it is reprojected back to man through the medium of the *hamingja*, formulated into the *fylgja*, and as such it conditions man's existence for the present and future. Although some of these points are not central to this thesis, they do indicate the intimate relationship between the *hamingja* and *fylgja*, and demonstrate the compulsory aspect of their function, which probably should not be understood separately from the aspect more central to the present study, which acts as a container of procreative power and potency.

Structural Analysis

At this point it is useful to venture a tentative "structure" of the soul, as it is conceived in Old Norse documents. The following discussion only includes the four aspects which have been treated above, and is therefore not intended to be an analysis of the Norse soul *in toto*, but it is hoped that it will serve to eliminate some of the confusion with regard to the distinctions between these four concepts, and to help differentiate them into basic functions, so that they may be used as reference points for further discussion. If we examine the functions of these entities, without reference to the various names which are attached to them, the following paradigm emerges:

I. Cognition/consciousness/will
II. Power/ability/luck (mobile)
III. Embodiment of personal power and action/obligation (attached)
IV. Embodiment of clanic power and action/obligation (attached)
V. "Character" (animal form)
VI. Semi-plastic image 'material '

These could certainly be further delineated but for purposes of the present work this analysis should suffice. Perhaps the special structural relationship between the *hamingja* and *fylgja* (referred to as the "*hamingja-fylgja* complex") should be summed up here. In the most common terminology, function II is the *hamingja* while function III is the (*manns-*)*fylgja*, and function IV is the *ættarfylgja*. Function II is a concrete, mobile form of magical power which may be separated from the individual in part or in its entirety and sent to other individuals at any time, while function III is a more specific development of this power which is coded to an individual and which may not be separated from that individual until death. Function IV is the development of function III through time and space, as it (III) attaches itself to a succession of individuals. Therefore, functions III and IV seem to be specific, personally and clanicly coded subsets of the more general and expansive function II. To one degree or another almost all of these functions (I-VI) are designated by anyone of the terms hugr, *hamingja*, *fylgja*, or *hamr* at one time or another in Old Norse documents. In the final analysis all of the above concepts and functions are closely interwoven and probably should best be understood as various aspects of the same basic "material."(64) The following discussion of **aftrburðr* attempts to clarify some of the distinctive characteristics, while demonstrating how these entities work in the rebirth process.

Rebirth

Previous ideas concerning the rebirth doctrine were outlined in Chapter II, however, here it would be useful to venture a general working theory at the outset of this section. Contrary to much of the earliest scholarship in this field, but generally in accordance with the work of M. Keil and others,(65) it is here suggested that the various name-giving practices were not the cause of rebirth, or an absolute indication of it, but rather that the two phenomena developed independently and later converged in mutual support until they became synonymous. The concept of rebirth, or *aftrburðr*,(66) probably developed at an early date, and later a variety of name-giving practices and rites developed which supported this belief. Technically, we are dealing with a transfer of *hamingja* and/or (*ættar-*)*fylgja* from one individual to another. In no way may this be interpreted to indicate "reincarnation" or immortality of the personality, in the popular modern sense. It is essentially the transfer of the *fylgja* (or the *hamingja-fylgja* complex), after the death of one individual, and before the birth of another, which is of the greatest interest to us here. However, it must also be kept in mind that certain aspects of this power (*hamingja*) could be transferred (in part) during the life of the "donor." These general beliefs were fairly common and consistent, while the naming customs varied widely over the centuries between the various Germanic tribes. The naming practices do, however, seem to play an extremely important role in this regard in Old Norse literature, and they are usually good indicators of rebirth themes, when this is not overtly stated.

Here, it is impossible to enter completely into the complex study of the many types of Germanic name-giving.(67) The various systems include alliteration, alliterative variation, thematic variation (the repetition of either the first or the last theme of the father's name), and simple *Nachbenennung*. The variation systems seem to be the oldest methods of naming children. and ones which are common to most of the Germanic tribes. It is probably that the pure variation method was most widely used at an early date by the continental tribes, however, it was probably also known in the north at an early period, since the two systems exist simultaneously in Iceland.(68) For purposes of this work it is important to realize that the two naming systems were essentially equivalent to one another, and that although the names of Sigmundr and Sigurðr perhaps historically stem from Frankish tradition, the contemporary Icelander would have

59

understood the connection between the two names quite well.(69) In fact, since the *fornaldarsaga* portrays events in semi-mythical times and locations, the somewhat more archaic system would be well suited to the genre.

At this point it seems appropriate to include some examples from genealogical tables in order to demonstrate the principles involved in these practices. The early genealogy of the Cheruscans shows the theme Sig- being inherited from father to son:

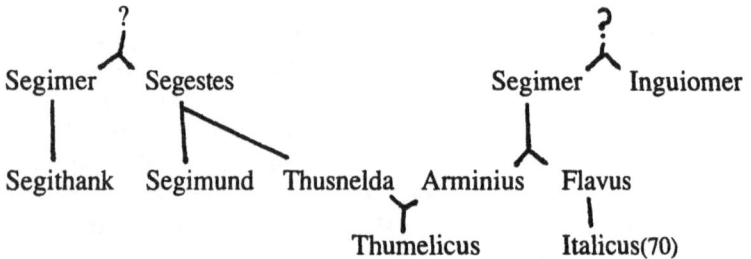

```
        ?                                    ?
       /\                                   /\
Segimer  Segestes              Segimer        Inguiomer
  |        |                        |
Segithank  Segimund  Thusnelda  Arminius  Flavus
                         Thumelicus        Italicus(70)
```

In the Icelandic tradition we can find examples of an interesting mixture of *Nachbenennung* and variation within the same geneology:

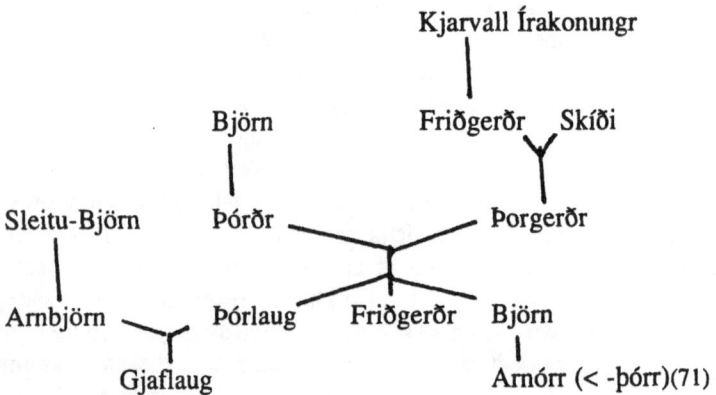

```
                              Kjarvall Írakonungr
                                      |
              Björn            Friðgerðr   Skíði
                |                      |
Sleitu-Björn   Þórðr                  Þorgerðr
    |                    \    /
Arnbjörn        Þórlaug   Friðgerðr  Björn
        Gjaflaug                      |
                                   Arnórr (< -þórr)(71)
```

60

The system of simple *Nachbenennung* was the most common and popular method in Iceland. The "Óðinic" *Egils saga* provides a good example:

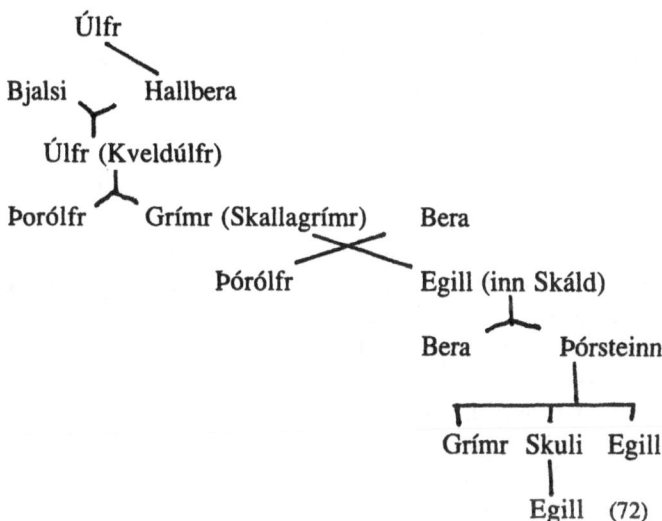

```
        Úlfr
          \
Bjalsi      Hallbera
        Y
   Úlfr (Kveldúlfr)
      人
Þorólfr    Grímr (Skallagrímr)    Bera
              Þórólfr   ×   Egill (inn Skáld)
                          人
                    Bera      Þorsteinn
                 ┌────────┬────────┐
               Grímr   Skuli    Egill
                         |
                       Egill   (72)
```

Here, it is evident that thematic variation continued to be an active factor even after *Nachbenennung* came to be the standard.

Apart from the determination that these two systems are essentially synonymous, it would be interesting to ascertain the unique psychological or conceptual nuances which form their foundations. For M. Keil, the reasons for this difference lies in the psychological realm. He believes that *Nachbenennung* belongs to a volitive-emotional sphere, while the variation system belongs to an affective-emotional sphere, and that the former is an expression of hope for a "lucky" future, while the latter expresses an effect of "*lebendigen Sprachempfinden.*" The name-variation is seen as a more visible, "artistic" expression of the same function, i.e., the "*Schicksalsleben,*" which connects the generations.(73) It is also possible that the variation system emphasizes the clan and its unity rather than the continuity of individual souls from generation to generation. The naming was itself a formalized ceremony which included the ritual formula known in Iceland as *vatni ausa*. This rite and its implications for the **aftrburðr* ideology will be discussed below in Chapters VII and VIII.

Although the question of an ancestor-worship cult (i .e., the ceremonial worship of ancestors) has sometimes been raised in connection with the rebirth theme, the naming practices, and the belief in "souls,"(74) there are in fact few instances in which rebirth has been overtly connected with the cultic worship of ancestors. It is probably true that the Germanic peoples had a developed ancestor cult,(75) but not one in which the personalities of individuals were worshiped. Rather, the ancestors seemed to have been melded into the realms of divine beings such as the *álfar* and *dísir*. Thus two "classes" of dead ancestors may be postulated: 1) those who will be reborn, and 2) those who are permanently disembodied and melded with semi-divine archetypes. Members of this latter group may aid in *aftrburðr*, however, they are not that which is reborn. References to sacrifices to known men are relatively rare and late, but not unknown.(76) For example, at one point in *Óláfs saga helga* the two ideas of ancestor cult and rebirth are juxtaposed.(77) Furthermore, the etymology of the OHG *eninchilî*: "the little ancestor" (= "grandson") points to the importance of the general concept of "the ancestor" and its importance over the whole of the Germanic territory.(78)

Before proceeding to the attestations of rebirth in Old Norse literature we should perhaps consider how the idea of rebirth relates to the belief in the various soul-entities outlined above. Only soul-functions II, III, and IV are said to be transferred from one person to another,(86) and only function II is said to be transferred during the life of the "sender." The transmission of a portion of the second function also constitutes a type of "rebirth," because it may be involved in initiatory paradigms. That is, it may describe a "passing of power" in order to bring the "receiver" (initiate) up to, or near the level of the "sender's" (master's) power. In this thesis we are mainly interested in the transmission of the totality of the transferable qualities from one individual to another, and it is this which we shall call *aftrburðr*. Thus, we are certainly dealing with the transference of the *hamingja* and *fylgja* in the cases of rebirth cited below, and perhaps in some cases, we may also see evidence of a transmission of other qualities such as the *hamr* or *hugr*.

The voluntary giving of a portion of one's *hamingja* is well attested in the saga literature. Here, it is considered a concrete power, or "luck" which may be granted to a person. Beliefs concerning this aspect of the *hamingja* were so strong that they survived well into the Christian era.(79) These are all instances in which the donor of the *hamingja* is still alive. However, there are also similar examples in which the donor is dead, and in his *haugr*. In *Göngu-Hrólfs saga* (ch. 32) the dead king, Hreggviðr says to his son-in-law, Hrólfr: "*Vildi ek til þín hyrfi öll sú hreysti ok hamingja, er mér hefir áðr fylgt*" (I want to turn all the courage and "luck" toward you, which formerly followed me).(80) In this type of *hamingja*-transfer the name of the recipient seems to matter little. The instance of *fylgja*-transfer cited above from *Hallfreðar saga* may have been influenced by the idea of the name drawing the *fylgja* to the person. The *hamingja*-transfer(81) found in *Víga-Glums saga*(82) also seems to belong to this class of "rebirth" in which the recipient is already born.

Now we shall enter upon the citation of various examples of "true" *aftrburðr* (or to coin another ON formula **fullaptrburðr*) drawn from several types of Old Norse documents. The mythological and heroic literature found in both the Eddic lays and in the *ESS* contain some overt and some obscure references to the doctrine of rebirth. The story of *ragnarök*, and the problems of the rebirth and/or the survival of the gods and men, is for the most part too complex to approach in detail here.(83) The *ragnarök* myth does, however, contain a theme which is at the very core of this thesis—that of vengeance. The "gods of vengeance," Váli and Víðarr, are said to survive the world-fire and re-emerge in the regenerated world.(84) Both of these gods are sons of Óðinn, and each was engendered to take vengeance. Váli was born from the union of Óðinn and Rindr in order to avenge the death of Baldr upon Höðr, and Víðarr was engendered in order to avenge his father upon the Fenrisúlfr.(85) Here, the idea of vengeance seems to be central to the rebirth or survival theme. It is also interesting to note that in the case of Váli, the god whom he avenged (Baldr), and the one upon whom he took his vengeance (Höðr), were also said to be reborn on the Iðavöllr.(86) Three other gods are specifically mentioned as surviving *ragnarök*: the sons of Þórr, Magni and Móði, as well as Hœnir, who apparently will return from Vanaheimr in the regenerated world.(87) The story of Gullveig in the "Völuspá" may also allude to some initiatory rebirth theme, but it does not appear central to our present considerations.(88) These mythological references present so many problems that each one would require lengthy discussion, which is

63

not possible here. It is important to realize that these myths do perhaps provide the paradigms for the rebirth ideology which we find expressed in the heroic literature and in the sagas, and most importantly to discern the central role which the act of vengeance seems to play in this motif. Since the story of Sigurðr is essentially heroic in character, it is generally within the realm of the heroic and family sagas that we will find the best examples of *aftrburðr* as it might relate to the Völsung-clan.

The most overt references concerning rebirth which occur in the Eddic literature appear in the Helgi-lays(89) and in the "Siguðarkviða in skamma."(90) From the latter we learn that it was indeed considered a good thing to be reborn in this world, because Högni curses Brynhildr by saying:

Letia maðr hána   *langrar gǫngo,*
þars hon aptrborin   *aldri verði!*

(May she not be prevented   from the long journey [to Hel] so that she may never be re-born.)

[Sg. 45.3-6]

It is from the Helgi-lays that the most explicit references occur. The final line of prose in the HHj. tells that Helgi Hjörvarðsson and his *valkyrja* Sváva were said to be reborn (*endrborin*), while the introductory prose to the HHII states that Sigmundr and Borghildr named their son, Helgi, after Helgi Hjörvarðsson. The final prose of the HHII reads: "*Þat var trúa í fornescio, at menn væri endrbornir, enn þat er nú kǫlluð kerlingavilla. Helgi oc Sigrún er kallat at væri endrborin.(89) Hét hann þá Helgi Haddingiascaði, enn hon Kára ...*" (It was believed in heathen times, that men were reborn, but that is now called an old wive's tale. Helgi and Sigrún are declared to have been reborn. He was called then Helgi Haddingjaskaði, and she [was called] Kara.) This Helgi Haddingjaskaði appears in the more historical *Ættartala frá Haud* of the *Flateyjabók*.(91) With regard to the Helgi-lays in general, it seems important that an identity of name(92) is maintained despite the fact that none of them are genetically related, and that the theme of vengeance is present throughout all the lays.(93) The similarities in style between the Helgi-lays and the Sigurðr-material make the possibility of the rebirth theme being present in the latter group even more tenable.

64

The *Fornaldarsögur* also present some examples of *aftrburðr*. It is said of Starkaðr Stórverksson that he was the eight-armed giant, Starkaðr, reborn (*endrborinn*).(94) The fact that Starkaðr (II) was born with eight arms, which Þórr ripped off, is evidence for a rebirth of the *hamr* as well as the usual *fylgja* and/or *hamingja*. That is, the image or form was reproduced, as well as the innate powers or qualities. Legends revolving around the name Haddingr (Saxo's Haddingus) also preserve a trace of a rebirth theme somewhat similar to that which we find in the Helgi-lays. In thē *Ættartala frá Haud*(95) we find that there was a series of three figures named Haddingr. However, in this case all we have are the names and various other mythical parallels with Saxo's Haddingus.(96)

The *Konungasögur* also contain several references to *aftrburðr* which are worthy of note. Perhaps the most famous of these is one involving Óláfr inn helgi. Upon seeing the grave mound of King Óláfr Geirstaðaálfr, St. Óláfr was asked by one of his warriors whether or not he (St. Óláfr) was buried there, for the people of Norway believed he was Óláfr Geirstaðaálfr reborn, but Óláfr answered that his spirit (*önd*) had never had two bodies, and never would.(97) Also connected to this legend is one concerning the birth of Óláfr inn helgi, in which the dead Óláfr Geirstaðaálfr appears to a certain Hrani in a dream and tells him to break into his *haugr* and after cutting off the head of the *draugr* (that of Óláfr himself), he is to take a ring, belt, and sword from the mound. Hrani was further instructed that he should take the belt and place it around the waist of Ásta, the pregnant wife of Hardr, the king of Greenland, and that their child should be named Óláfr. Also the ring and the sword were to be given to the boy as gifts from Óláfr Geirstaðaálfr.(98) The original Óláfr Geirstaðaálfr was in fact a distant ancestor of St. Óláfr.

In the *Sturlungasaga* we find convincing evidence that the belief in the inheritance of qualities and *ørlög* through naming practices was still current, despite the seemingly thorough "Christianization" of the people by this time.(99) The hero Kolbeinn Tumason died in 1208 at the age of thirty-five, and soon thereafter a son was born to Þórvaldr Gizurarson. All the people advised Þórvaldr to name his son after the great Kolbeinn, but he refused, saying that *vitrir menn* had told him that men should not name their sons after men who had been "called from the world" early. In 1210, a son was born to Arnórr Tumason, the brother of Kolbeinn. Arnórr named the boy Kolbeinn and he became a powerful chieftain, but in 1245, when he was thirty-five years old, Kolbeinn inn yngri died. He was buried beside Kolbeinn inn eldri.(100) This example is especially interesting due to the "fate" aspect, and the historical orientation of the saga.

The *Íslendingasögur* contain a large number of passages which could be cited as examples of the rebirth theme. Many of these instances involve the passing of the name as the central motif, as for example, in the *Svarfdœla saga* ch. 5. Here, a certain Þorólfr asks his brother to name a son after him if he should die, so that his name will not pass away. With the name, Þorólfr would give the boy all the luck (*heillir*) which had followed him in life. These motifs are quite common in the Sagas of the Icelanders and Kings' Sagas,(101) however, there is one particularly interesting instance found in the *Þórðar saga hreðu* (*Brot eldri gerðar*). In this saga we read how a certain Bárekr kills Þórðr by wounding him on the left arm with a poisoned sword.(102) The complete saga relates that at the funeral feast a son was born to Helga, the wife of Þórðr, and he was named Þórðr after his father.(103) It was noticed that the baby had a scar on his left arm in exactly the same place where his father had been wounded.(104) As with Starkaðr, this may be an example of a reborn *hamr* as well as *hamingja-fylgja*.

From the evidence above, we may venture a typology of rebirth (transference of a spiritual quality or entity) along a three-fold paradigm, thusly:

	Donor	→	Recipient	Transferred function
I	living	→	living	Function II
II	dying/dead	→	living	Functions II, II I and/or IV
III	dying/dead	→	unborn	Functions II, II I and/or IV, and perhaps other functions

It is the third of these types which is central to this work, and which could be called "*fullaftrburðr*."

Funeral Customs

Because the phenomenon of death is so tightly interwoven with that of rebirth, it seems necessary to delve into the "world of the dead" to some degree. Although this area of study may not provide the major keys to the understanding of the belief in *aftrburðr*,(105) it does provide a necessary context for general beliefs concerning the dead and their place in the universe.

Essentially, we find two major types of funeral rites, inhumation and cremation, with a third and rarer subtype, the "ship-funeral."(106) Inhumation was the oldest method of disposing of the dead used by the Indo-European peoples, and it continued uncontested until the Bronze Age when the custom of cremation was introduced. This is also true for the Germanic branch of the Indo-European culture. During the Roman period the custom of inhumation returned to the north, and the two methods existed side by side until the coming of Christianity, at which time cremation was excluded.(107) Principally, we are interested in this period of mixed customs. All types of funeral customs included offerings of various types which were either buried with the dead (whether the body was burned or not) or the burning of the objects with the body. Very often the burial would include a complete ship. From this evidence it is clear that these people believed in a continued existence of some sort, and the practice of cremation seems to indicate a belief that the "soul" could continue to exist without the body. But was this an existence in some "other-world," or was it here in this world, or both? Also, was the burning of the dead inspired by spiritual considerations, or by fear of the *aptrgöngumaðr*? It is hoped that the following discussion may shed some light on these two questions.

The ship-funeral, in which the body was placed in a ship and set adrift (sometimes aflame) is attested in some literary sources(108) and seems to indicate a belief in some other-world across the sea (perhaps to the west).(109) Faced with this, and the various other practices mentioned above, the question must be asked: Where do the dead go and what is the nature of their destination? The literature knows of several destinations for the dead, principally they are Valhöll or Hel, however, other abodes such as Niflhel or Fólkvangr (the hall to which Freyja takes her share of the fallen warriors)(110) are also known. The grave-mound (ON *haugr*) itself is often described as a small world of the dead, one in which the *draugr* exists as an animated corpse.(111) The belief that the dead went into mountains or hills, such as the Helgafell in Iceland, was also apparently widespread.(112) To these conceptions we must of course add the now well attested belief in rebirth. The problem of the survival of the personality, or self, is still present. However, it seems more likely that if the personality were to survive, it would survive in one of these other-worlds rather than in a reborn form. Essentially, it appears that we are dealing with three, types, or classes of "abodes" for the dead: 1) the other-world, be it Valhöll, Hel, Niflhel, Fólkvangr, or any other apparently metaphysical realm; 2) the grave-mound, where the *draugr* of a person may continue to be active for a time; and 3) this world, through rebirth within the tribe or clan (aftrburðr í ætt).(113) This analysis is by no means intended to be complete with reference to the complexity of relationships between these various worlds, or realms of being, but rather it is merely intended to serve as a convenient classification of basic types for purposes of this study.

This multiple type of conception is not rare among peoples adhering to traditional religious forms,(114) and in fact the earlier portion of this chapter provides a metaphysic of the soul which could account for, or accommodate, these various beliefs for the Germanic peoples. It would be my guess that the diverse aspects or functions(115) of the soul "survive" death in various abodes or states of being. The first function could continue to exist in one of the other-worlds; the sixth function could exist for a time in a semi-conscious state in the *haugr*, while either one or all of functions II, II, or IV could be reborn in the flesh of a descendant. This phenomenon of *multiprésence*(116) or poly-psyche indeed seems to be a key to the best answer to the question concerning the "destination of the dead."

The motivations behind the cremation of the dead, and the relationships between this practice and the ideology of *aftrburðr* are less certain. There has been no completely satisfactory answer given to these questions; however, we may be able to shed some light on these problems by observing the phenomena from a "techno-metaphysical' view-point, i.e., through "technical" aspects of the soul conceptions. In the period between the Bronze Age and the Roman Age, when cremation was the primary form of funeral custom, there was probably a belief in rebirth of one type or another,(117) and there was also most certainly the belief in the *aptrgöngumaðr*. Therefore, it would seem that in this period the funeral customs were designed to prevent the "walking-dead," but at the same time this would not hinder, and perhaps it would aid, the "rebirth' of the dead person into this and/or another world. This may indicate that the people of this period believed in a stronger link between the sixth soul function, which could re-animate a corpse, and the other soul functions. If they thought that the animating principle could drag the other aspects of the soul back to the grave with it, thus preventing the rebirth of those qualities, then the use of cremation in this regard would become clearer. It may be that they not only wanted to prevent the dangers of the *aptrgöngumaðr*, but also to facilitate *aftrburðr*. Generally, it seems that at least for the north Germanic peoples there was little trace of a conception of the *aptrgöngumaðr* or *draugr* as a morally evil being—merely dangerous. For in may cases this was the *draugr* of a beloved ancestor. In this regard we are reminded of the curious episode in *Óláfs saga helga* in which the *fylgja* of Óláfr Geirstaðaálfr comes to Hrani in a dream and advises him to kill the *draugr* (corpse animated by the *hamr*) of none other than Óláfr himself! The destruction of the original body to which it had a natural proclivity to return, would then send the "soul" in search of a new, "soulless' form, i.e., that of an unborn child. Because the soul would have a natural proclivity for its own kind, its own ætt, it would probably enter a child belonging to its clan. The name, or naming-rite could act as a magical agent in this regard.(118) In later times, when burial existed contemporaneously with cremation, it seems likely that the Germanic peoples had developed a more intense sense of *multiprésence*. That is, they perhaps believed that the soul functions were less likely to hinder one another after death; that they could go their separate ways, and that this was perhaps not undesirable. All of this is quite speculative, but it does seem to have a basis in the "rationale" behind the metaphysic of the Germanic soul. The general respect and admiration expressed by the Germanic peoples for the concepts "ancestor" and "kin," at all levels of their culture (political, religious), would tend to indicate that the motivation for such practices as cremation are to be found more in magico-religious considerations rather than in instinctual *fears* concerning the dead.

The lack of rigid religious dogma among the Germanic tribes makes final conclusions concerning the funeral customs and the belief in rebirth quite difficult. Most scholars seem to think that the variations in funeral practices do not necessarily indicate a variation in the conception of the soul, or in the belief in an afterlife or rebirth.(119) As we have seen each method may be adapted to these beliefs. The key to understanding these customs seems not to lie so much in the conceptions of afterlife, or of various gods, but rather in the shifting of emphases and nuances within an already loosely, yet commonly, agreed upon metaphysical paradigm.

In this section concerning the doctrine of rebirth we have noted the various soul functions and how they appear to operate in the

Germanic world, alone, and with regard to *aptrburðr*. We have also seen how naming practices and other cultic considerations are connected to a belief in rebirth. The importance of the "rite" of vengeance was also briefly touched upon with regard to Víðarr and Váli, a theme which is discussed further in Chapters VII and VIII below. The acts of vengeance by these divine progeny perhaps describe the mythical exemplary model for a theme found in the *Völsungasaga*. The world of the gods is always in close proximity to all of the Völsungar, because they are in fact direct descendants of the god Óðinn. This section has dealt with the rebirth of qualities from one human generation to the next; the next deals with the transmission from a god to man.

Germanic Divine Progenitorship

A theme central to the story of Sigurðr, and more particularly to the whole *Völsungasaga* is the descent from the god, Óðinn. He founds the dynasty with Sigi, and he recharges and reinvigorates it with Völsungr. Generally, within the Germanic world we find that the gods are the founders of whole clans, tribes or even entire social classes, and it is this function which is strongly emphasized. While the role of a god as a direct *Heldenvater* of individual heroes, e.g., the type we find most often in Greece or Ireland, is not the rule in the Germanic territories.(120) In the Germanic realms it is less likely that the first son of the god on earth will be great, than it is that the last or ultimate son in the line will manifest the highest degree of greatness. The human element, and earthly experiences seem to add to, rather than dilute the divine power.

Before proceeding to some examples of divine fatherhood in Germanic myth and legend, we should perhaps examine the technical aspects of this phenomenon within the context of the previously presented material concerning rebirth. It would seem correct to venture that the progeny of a god on earth was considered in some degree to be the god reborn. But not the god himself since the divinity is not "dead" nor subject to the same laws to which humanity is bound with regard to death.(121) The hero only inherits a portion of the god's power (*hamingja*) upon which he may build an edifice of honor through his accomplishments, thus adding to his "personal" *hamingja*, or perhaps more completely manifesting the divine force allotted to him. Especially in the case of Óðinic heroes it seems that the god imparts not only the power, or *hamingja*, but that he also

70

"personally" aids them, and usually has one of the *valkyrjur* follow and protect the hero as well. It is difficult to venture any more concerning the metaphysical technicalities of this phenomenon since we do not have enough examples which are commented upon in any detail by the old sagamen, as is the case with the soul conceptions and rebirth, within the simple, human context.

The belief in divine progenitorship also provides some more evidence for the existence of the concept of "ancestor worship" in the Germanic world. If the gods were in fact considered to be the ancestors of mankind, and they were indeed worshiped, then we may characterize this as a basic form of ancestor cult, from which other concepts may have emerged at a later time.

Many of the tribal names of the Germanic peoples are derived from the names of mythical figures.(122) There are essentially two types of divine progenitorship expressed in Germanic tradition: 1) the god who fathers mankind in general, or the gamut of social classes, etc.; and 2) the god who founds clans and dynasties (which eventually become tribes). *Germania* (ch. 2) provides us with an excellent example of the first type. There Tacitus states that the Germans "*celebrant ... Tuistonem deum terra editum et filium Mannum originem gentis conditoresque.*" He further states that Mannus had three sons, from whom the names of the tribes (*gentes*) were derived, i.e., the Ingaevones, the Herminones, and the Istaevones.(123) He also says that they believe many more of the tribal names are derived from the names of other sons of Mannus. O. Höfler sees a specific pattern in this myth; that of the "forefather – son – three sons of the son."(124) This may be seen repeated elsewhere in Germanic myth and legend in varying states of preservation. The Eddic material also provides us with an example of a god founding humanity and its social institutions. In the "Rígsþula" we read of Rígr (= Heimdallr) who, while walking in Miðgarðr, engendered three sons with three different women. With Edda (great-grandmother) he begot Þræll (thrall), with Amma (grandmother) he begot Karl (freeman), and with Móðir (mother) he begot Jarl (earl)(125) Rígr undertakes the education of Jarl, teaching him runes and war-wisdom. It is again interesting to note that it is the youngest, the ultimate son who is the most powerful. This theme is again repeated in the "Rígsþula" when Jarl has two sons, Kundr (the older), and Konr (the younger). Konr was the only one who possessed runic (numinous) knowledge and thus ascended to the title "Rígr," which

71

his father, Jarl, had also won before him.(126) This is quite in keeping with the evolutionary theme which is evident in the rebirth tradition, as discussed above. This seems to belong more to the religious world of numinous knowledge and initiation rather than to the world of social law in which primogeniture was the rule. J. Fleck also indicates the possibility that Heimdallr-Rígr is a hypostasis of Óðinn,(127) and this would of course fit quite with with Rígr's functions in the "Rígsþula" as both a progenitor of men (Óðinn : Alfaðir) and a dispenser of numinous knowledge (Óðinn : Ginnarr).

Óðinn is also one of the most prominent founders of royal dynasties and heroic clans. The Anglo-Saxon genealogies show the royal houses of Kent, East Anglia, Essex, Mercia and Wessex all traced back to Wōden.(128) The most famous of all the Óðinic clans is that of the Völsungar. This is of course explicitly stated in the *Völsungasaga*, however, the names of the various heroes in the Völsung-line also re-emphasize this. The names "Völsi" (→ Völsungr = the son of Völsi [= son of Óðinn]) and Sigmundr are attested *Óðinsheiti*. Therefore, not only is Óðinn the founder of the line, his influence is strongly felt throughout the development of the clan. It is also worthy of note that the theme *sig-* is a frequent one in *Óðinsheiti*, e.g., Sigðir, Siggautr, Sigtryggr, Sig-Týr, and Sigfaðir.(129) This would re-emphasize the nature of Sigi, the first "Völsung." Other clans receive their names from other known gods, such as the Ynglingar from Yngvi (= Freyr)(130) and the Skjöldungar from Skjöldungr.(131) There are many other examples, but most may be eventually traced to one of the major Æsir or Vanir.

From the wide distribution and ancient attestations of this tradition we may conclude that the concept of divine progenitorship was indeed indigenous to the Germanic tradition,(132) and that this played an important part in old Germanic mythology. The idea behind the many hypostases of Óðinn is perhaps one quite akin to that of rebirth. These hypostases are the god, but at the same time they represent functional emanations or descendants of him. In a cultic sense the names are meant to represent a religious view which has many aspects.(133) This concept is important to this thesis because it helps reveal the true nature of Sigurðr.

Footnotes to Chapter Five

1. For purposes of this study the term "soul" is used as a generic designation for what may be considered "non-physical" portions of the psychosomatic, or mind-body, complex.

2. Cf. E. Meyer (1891), 61 ff; W. Golther (1895), 72 ff; P. D. C. de la Saussaye (1902),289 ff; P. Hermann (1903), 31 ff; K. Helm (1913), I, 17 ff; J. de Vries (1937), II, 348 ff; J. de Vries (1956), I, 217 ff.

3. Cf. V. Grönbech (1931); M. Keil (1931); K. Eckhardt (1937); J. de Vries (1956); H. R. E. Davidson (1943); E. Mundal (1974).

4. For difficulties in translation of ancient concepts, cf. L. Gruber (1977), 330 ff.

5. E. Polomé (1969), 268-269.

6. R. Cleasby and G. Vigfusson (1957),290. See also the many compounds and derivations.

7. V. Grönbech (1931), 1,108.

8. *Harðar saga ok Hólmverja* ch. 31.

9. J. de Vries (1956), 1,220-221; D. Strömbäck (1975),17 ff.

10. Cf. Go. *hugs*: "intellect," used by Wulfila to translate Greek νους; OHG *hugu* "spirit, mind"; OE *hyge*: "thought, soul"; OS *hugi* "spirit; soul"; O.Fris. *hei*: "mind, spirit."

11. J. de Vries (1956), I, 221.

12. V. Grönbech (1931), 1,250.

13. D. Strömbäck (1975), 17 ff.

14. R. Cleasby and G. Vigfusson (1957),236, and J. de Vries (1961), 208.

15. J. de Vries (1956), I, 222-223.

16. V. Grönbech (1931), 1,264.

17. Cf. *Yngl.* ch. 7; *Hrólfs s. kr.* ch. 33.

18. E. Mundal (1974),38 ff., and V. Grönbech (1931), 1,264.

19. Cf. *Friðjólfs saga* ch. 6.

20. J. de Vries (1956), 1,223.

21. J. de Vries (1956), 1,224.

22. J. Grimm (1966), II,728-730.

23. Both *gæfa* and *gipt(a)* are derived from the verbal root meaning "to give" → "that which is given" → "gift" → "luck" (cf. beliefs concerning the "giving" of *hamingja*, etc.). *Heill* originally was purely part of the sacred vocabulary, but in ON it also carries the adjectival sense of "whole" or "complete," while the noun means "omen , good luck."

24. J. de Vries (1956), I, 224, and E. Mundal (1974),86 ff.

25. U. Holmberg (1964), 11.

26. This word is used in the sense A. van Gennep uses it in *The Rites of Passage*, i.e., non-animistic, more similar to the "mana" concept.

27. See R. Cleasby and G. Vigfusson (1957), 236. The phrase literally means "to lay one's luck on someone." Cf. also the various other expressions cited there.

28. This passage is of considerable importance when we consider the role of the *hamingja* in the rebirth process.

29. *Víga-Glums saga* ch. 6. See Ch. VII for parallels for the sword-gift as a sign of *hamingja* transfer.

30. H. Falk (1926), 171, and J. de Vries (1956), 1,222.

31. G. Dumézil (1970),142.

32. V. Grönbech (1931), 1,285; cf. *Hálfdanar saga svarta.*

33. V. Grönbech (1931), 1,299-300; cf. also K. Eckhardt (1937), 114-117 concerning the role of the mother in the rebirth of the soul.

34. V. Grönbech (1931), I, 307-08.

35. This complex of ideas is well discussed by F. Kaufmann (1926), 397 ff. and is probably best understood in light of the investigations of P. Bauschatz, see P. Bauschatz (1975),53 ff. Here the possibility of linking the concept of *ørlög* with that of *hamingja* is quite tempting.

36. V. Grönbech (1931), 1,286.

37. Cf. E. Mundal (1974),26 ff. for a complete analysis of these two motifs. (The female-*fylgja* is reborn, while the animal-*fylgja* is not.)

38. J. de Vries (1956), I, 224-227 and H. Falk (1926), 169 ff.

39. P. Hermann (1903), 80.

40. J. de Vries (1961a), 147-148.

41. V. Grönbech (1931), 11,247-248.

42. P. D. C. de la Saussaye (1902),293. An example of this is found in the *Hallfreðar saga* discussed in this chapter.

43. Cf. the *Víga-Glums saga* discussed in this chapter, and the parallels given in Ch. VII.

44. Cf. HHj and *Njáls saga* ch. 62.

45. Cf. the essentially heathen contexts of most of the other instances of *fylgja* or *hamingja* transfer, and the concept of *aftrburðr*, which would most certainly not be derived from orthodox Christian sources.

46. J. de Vries (1956), I, 228.

47. This too seems to be an essentially pagan belief grafted into Christian ideology.

48. Cf. *Þiðranda þáttr* (= *Flb.* 1,419 ff.) where we hear of nine women in dark clothing coming from the north, and nine in bright clothing from the south—the dark ones kill Þiðrandi and claim him as a sacrifice for the old faith.

49. J. de Vries (1956), I, 227.

50. W. Golther (1895), 98; cf. also the term *fylgjur* in HHj prose following st. 34, and the similar conception concerning the *hamingjur* outlined in this chapter.

51. J. de Vries (1956), 1,226.

52. V. Grönbech (1931), II, 248.

53. E. O. G. Turville-Petre (1964), 221 ff. and H. R. Davidson (1946), 130 ff.

54. Cf. relevant passages in HHj., HHI, and HHII.

55. Cf. Vkv., opening prose and sts. 1-5. Here it is described how Völundr and his brothers Slagfriðr and Egill meet three *valkyrjur* at Úlfdalr and subsequently they are all married to one another. After seven years the *valkyrjur* fly away to battle. Egill and Slagfriðr set out after their lost wives, only Völundr stays behind and does not seek Hervör alvitr.

56.   Cf. Vkv. st. 17 ff.

57.   W. Golther (1895), 98-99.

58.   P. D. C. de la Saussaye (1902), 293.

59.   See note 62 below.

60.   Cf. *Víga-Glums saga* and various other examples given in this chapter and in Ch. VII.

61.   J. de Vries (1956), 1, 228.

62.   P. Bauschatz (1975), 56 ff. Here, the cosmic laws are described in a way very similar to the way in which old Gmc. laws (and in many cases modern laws) function, i.e., by the principle of precedent.

63.   P. Bauschatz (1975).

64.   The etymological and semantic interweave of these diverse concepts have already been pointed out in this chapter.

65.   M. Keil (1931),97 ff. and G. Flom (1917), 7 ff., and H. R. Davidson (1943), 138 ff.

66.   The noun *aftrburðr* never occurs in that exact form the texts, however, the participle *aptrborinn* is common, from which the noun *aftrburðr* is derived.

67.   Excellent studies in this field have been provided by G. Flom (1917) for early Gmc., and by M. Keil for Icelandic; see also others cited in Chapter 11.

68.   M. Keil (1931), 1 ff.

69.   Cf. especially the many examples given by M. Keil (1931), 60 ff.; 6-26, concerning the contemporary mixing of variation and Nachbenennung, and evidence presented there concerning the thematic variation system in Iceland.

70.   K. Eckhardt (1937), 59.

71.   M. Keil (1931), 62.

72.   K. Eckhardt (1937), 27.

73.   M. Keil (1931), 108.

74.   W. Gother (1895), 93 ff., H. Falk (1926), 173.

75.   W. Gother (1895), 94., E. O. G. Turville-Petre (1963), 201., cf. also Jordanes ch. 13 and Adam of Bremen ch. 26.

76.   Cf. E. Birkili (1938), 86 ff. for a list of examples.

77.   Cf. *Óláfs saga helga* ch. 7 (= *Flb.* II, 7), this passage is discussed in detail in this chapter. Evidence for an ancestor cult involving the *álfar* and *dísir* is discussed by E. O. G. Turville-Petre (1964), 221 ff., and (1963), 201; and H. Falk (1926), 172.

78.   J. de Vries (1956), I, 218.

79.   For a number of examples for this use of the *hamingja*, cf. H. R. Davidson (1946), 132 ff. and R. Cleasby and G. Vigfusson (1957), 236 under the entry "*hamingja.*"

80.   Cf. *Göngu-Hrólfs saga* ch. 32.

81.   In this instance the term *hamingja* seems to describe the third and/or fourth soul functions.

82.   See text cited in this chapter.

83.   Cf. relevant literature in J. Martin (1972), 133 ff. and G. Storm (1893), 222.

84. Cf. passages concerning the vengeance of Víðarr (Vsp. 53) and of Váli (Bdr. 11), and their "rebirth" in Vm. 51.

85. We will return to the myths of Víðarr and Váli in Ch. VII.

86. For evidence concerning the rebirth of Baldr and Höðr cf. Vsp. 61 and *ESS* 41 (53), where it is said: "*koma þar Balldr ok Haudr fa Heliar.*"

87. Cf. Vsp. 62 and Vm. 51.

88. See Vsp. 21.

89. See note 54 above.

90. Cf. Sg. 45. This poem probably originated in 11th- or 12th-century Iceland.

91. Cf. *Flb.* I, 24.

92. The name "Helgi" is actually an adjectival noun meaning "the holy one," and may even be regarded as a title rather than as a proper name. See O. Höfler (1952), 164.

93. In the HHj. Helgi avenges his *móðirfaðir*, and in the HHI and HHII the vengeance of Helgi on the Hundingssynir for the death of his father (Sigmundr) is central.

94. *Gautreks saga* ch. 7.

95. See note 91 above.

96. Cf. also G. Dumézil (1973), 9 ff. and ch. VII.

97. Cf. *Flb.* II, 135. The term *önd*, along with *sál*, became the words most used by Christians to translate the Latin terms *spiritus* and *anima* respectively.

98. Cf. *Flb.* II, 7-9.

99. The *Sturlunga saga* is the latest of the Icelandic Family Sagas. It was written contemporaneously with the age about which it was written. It concerns the time between 1117 and ca. 1260, and it was composed between ca. 1230 and ca. 1340.

100. Cf. *Sturlunga saga* 1, 284 and II, 84 *et passim*.

101. For more examples cf. K. Eckhardt (1937), 10 ff., H. R. Davidson (1946),141 ff., P. Hermann (1903), 35 ff.

102. See *Þórðar s. hr.* (Brot.) ch. 3.

103. See *Þórðar s. hr.* ch. 1.

104. See *Þórðar s. hr.* (*Brot*) ch. 3. M. Keil (1931), 79; 91 defends the authenticity of this saga as a source for the study of rebirth and naming practices.

105. See conclusions in this chapter.

106. This is closely connected with, but should in some respects be kept distinct from the ship-burial or the use of a ship as the funeral pyre, as seen in the text of Ibn Fadlan's *Travel Report*.

107. For a good review of these customs in the context of religious history, see H. R. Davidson (1946), 7 ff.

108. Cf. *Bēowulf* 50-52, and the *Ynglinga saga* ch. 23, also the story of King Sigurðr Hringr in the *Sjöldunga saga*.

109. This would parallel some Celtic beliefs concerning the "other-world."

110. Cf. "Grímnismál" 14.

111. H. R. Davidson (1946),90 ff.

112. W. v. Unwerth (1911), 17 ff.

113. Cf. J. de Vries (1956), I, 218.

114. Cf. E. Birkeli (1938), 11-16 concerning *multiprésence*.

115. See the discussion of "soul-functions" in this chapter.

116. Cf. Lucien Lévy-Bruhl, *L'ame Primitive* (Paris, 1927), 427-429.

117. This would be true if J. de Vries (1956; 1961b) and K. Eckhardt (1937) and others are correct in assuming that this phenomenon is part of the common IE heritage, or at least common to both the Celtic and Gmc. branches of that culture.

118. Cf. also K. Eckhardt (1937), 124-125.

119. J. de Vries (1956), I, 217, H. R. Davidson (1946), 61 ff.; cf. also K. Eckhardt (1937), 121 ff.

120. See Ch. VI for parallels.

121. The gods may be killed, but apparently they may also be reborn, as delineated in the myth of *ragnarök*.

122. See O. Höfler (1973), 19 ff. for some examples of these.

123. The first two of these names may be derived from known god names: "Herminones" is paralleled by the Saxon name *Irmin-got*, and "Ingaevones" is paralleled in the god names Ing and Yngvi. The third remains unexplained.

124. O. Höfler (1973),19. Cf. for example the *ESS* 5(6), where the pattern is apparent:

Buri
|
Borr
┌──────┼──────┐
Óðinn Vili Vé

125. Note that the descending ages of the mothers corresponds with the ascending power of their offspring.

126. For an excellent study of this theme of numinous knowledge, the youngest son, and kingship, see J. Fleck (1970), 39 ff.

127. J. Fleck (1971b), 401., E. O. G. Turville-Petre (1964), 154 ff. doubts that Heimdallr is a son of Óðinn, however, if Fleck is correct this would be irrelevant.

128. Cf. J. Grimm (1966), 1709 ff.

129. Cf. H. Falk (1924), 25-26.

130. Cf. the *Ynglinga saga* ch. 9. Freyr was in turn the son of Njörðr, see *Ynglinga saga* ch. 4.

131. Cf. prose introduction to the "Grottasöngr" [= S. Bugge (1867), 324] where we read: "Skjöldr hét sonr Oþins."

132. O. Höfler (1973), 20-21.

133. O. Höfler (1973), 23; cf. also "Grímnismál" 54.

CHAPTER SIX

REBIRTH IDEOLOGIES IN OTHER TRADITIONS

The rebirth doctrine also appears in several other Indo-European and non-Indo-European religious traditions. It is necessary to discuss a number of these in order to place the Germanic traditions in proper context and perspective.

Indo-European Traditions

Of all Indo-European peoples, it is among the Celts that we find the most numerous parallels to the Germanic type of belief in *aftrburðr*. However, there are many important contrasts between these two "systems" as well. Some of these variations could possibly be attributed to the zeal with which the early Christian monks, scribes for these Celtic works, expurgated all references to "reincarnation" from the stories of the old Celtic hero-gods.(1) Legends still exist which are largely predicated upon a rebirth ideology, and which sometimes contain explicit references to the idea of rebirth.

The conceptions of the soul among the Celts was apparently somewhat similar to that found among the Germanic peoples. For example, the dead could exist in various abodes after death, they could remain in the burial-mound (OIr. *síd*), go to the "otherworld,"(2) or be reborn into the world of men, all simultaneously.(3) Generally, the Celtic divine-hero tales do not provide us with the relatively well rounded picture we get from the combination of Germanic sagas and Eddas. It is difficult to ascertain exactly what the common beliefs were concerning the souls of the normal human being, when most of the documentation concerns the semi-divine hero. Also, the ideology of divine progenitorship was extremely well developed in Celtic mythology. Most of the major heroes or heroines were considered to be the sons and daughters of the gods, or to be the gods themselves reborn on the earth. This is much more akin to the Greek type of *Heldenvater* than to the Germanic ~*ættarfaðir* mentioned earlier. The function of this phenomenon will be apparent in the examples provided below.

The Cú Chulainn cycle presents us with a classic example of divine progenitorship. After an interlude of three years in the síd, Dechtire bears a son named Setanta (later renamed "Cú Chulainn"). The God Lug is the actual father of the boy, although Sualtach, the mortal husband of Dechtire claims him. Cú Chulainn always remains conscious of his divine origin. This motif is the most common found in the Irish rebirth tales: a divine member of the *síd*-mound, and one of the Tuatha Dé Danann, is the father of a "mortal" child and at the same time he is incarnated in the child. It is unclear whether the god continues to exist in the *síd* during this period of incarnation. However, the Cú Chulainn cycle also provides an example of a second motif which is perhaps more important for an analysis of the idea of the transmigration of the soul, as it was believed to exist in a more general religio-cultural context, separated from the direct influence of the *síd* and its divine inhabitants. In the *Tochmarc Emire* (Wooing of Emer) we find a passage which tells of the desire of the Ulstermen that Cú Chulainn find a wife and produce an heir as soon as possible, because of their fear that he would perish early. They wished for this heir: "*Ar ro fetatar is uad fessin no biad a athgein*" (knowing that his rebirth would be of himself).(4) This can easily be compared to the third incarnation of Etain. In the Etain cycle(5) we find what is perhaps the best example of the Celtic concept, because the tale spans three generations of rebirths. The third of these is the daughter of the second, and they all bear the same name. Originally, Etain is divine, and the wife of the god, Midir, in the *síd*-mound. Subsequently she is incarnated as Etain, the daughter of Etar, king of Echrad. In this form she marries Eochaid, king of Tara. Etain, the wife of Eochaid, then bears one daughter, also named Etain. The cycle of Finn mac Cumaill may also contain a vestigial rebirth motif. In the *Macgnimartha Find* we find the theme of the posthumous son who becomes a great hero. Cumaill is killed in battle leaving his wife pregnant with his seventh son. When the boy is born he is secretly fostered and nurtured in a remote forest area. Later the king of Bantry, into whose service Finn anonymously enters, says: "*Dia facbad Cumull mac andar limm ro bo tu-sa é. Acht cena ní cualamar-ne d'facbail do acht Tulcha mac Cumaill*" (If Cumall had left a son I would think you were he. But we have not heard of his leaving [one] except Tulcha son of Cumall).(6) It is also implied that ˜Mongan mac Manannan was a rebirth of Finn mac Cumaill "*acht nad leic a forndisse*" (though he would not let it be told).(7) The relatively casual and obscure statements concerning Cú Chulainn and Finn are perhaps the most reliable evidence for a common belief in rebirth among the Celts, because these passages do not seem to be a part of any literary reworking or conventionalism.

J. de Vries believes that there was a Celtic prototype of the belief in rebirth, and that this doctrine consisted of an ideology of *polypsychê* and the rebirth of one of those souls within the archaic clanic structure.(8) The Celtic system provides another important feature, besides the emphasis on divine progenitorship, which distinguishes it from the Germanic ideology, or their supposedly common Indo-European prototype. The role of women, especially in the process of divine progenitorship, is of extreme importance. In fact the woman was considered to be the vehicle by which the gods and/or the dead were reborn generation after generation, and the human husband was usually regarded as being of little spiritual consequence.(9) The statements concerning Cú Chulainn and Finn seem to contradict the absolute hegemony of this idea. Also characteristic of the Celtic doctrine is the central position assumed by the *síd*-mound. This is the doorway through which the living pass to the dead and the dead return to the living. It is also the home of the Tuatha Dé Danann, the divine figures who are the source of the great heroes. The *síd* is somewhat analogous to the role which Hel (Niflhel) and the *haugr* have played in the Germanic system. Many of the early classical authors writing about the Celts reported that they held the teaching of Pythagoras called metempsychosis.(10) This seems to have been a philosophical *interpretatio Romana* or *Graeca*. Most scholars now contend that the Celtic rebirth ideology is basically of internal origin.(11) Before J. de Vries, Karl Eckhardt proposed the idea of a common Indo-European rebirth ideology, which would accommodate the later developments of this doctrine within the Indo-European cultural sphere.

The Thracian myth of Zalmoxis was also connected with the Pythagorean doctrine of metempsychosis by Herodotus (IV: 95-96) when writing about the Getae, a Thracian tribe. Later commentators were to elaborate upon this connection. In more recent times, E. Rohde speculated that the Thracians did indeed believe in a doctrine of soul transmigration, and that the Greeks quickly interpreted this to be identical to the teachings of their own philosopher, Pythagoras. However, Rohde indicates that the Thracian doctrine probably developed independently from the Pythagorean teaching.(12) K. Eckhardt follows Rohde in most respects, and further develops the idea that the Pythagorean and Thracian systems were genetically related Indo-European beliefs.(13) The most complete study of this problem has been provided by M. Eliade,(14) who is not so quick to conclude that the myth of Zalmoxis represents a doctrine of reincarnation, since this is not explicitly stated in the texts. On the other hand, Eliade is impressed by the *interpretio Graeca* of the Zalmoxian doctrine as that of Pythagoras, and he concludes that the Thracians must have certainly held a belief in the immortality of the soul. Other sources allude to the common Thracian belief in the return of the dead.(15) All modern scholars agree that the myth of Zalmoxis is more archaic than the philosophical teachings of Pythagoras.

In Greece we find a wealth of evidence indicative of a belief in rebirth, from the mystery religions to the philosophy of Pythagoras.(16) The earliest Pythagorean system probably only knew of the reincarnation of humans in human form. It is said of Pythagoras that he was reborn ten to twenty times, all in human form. In later times, however, a system developed wherein the human being could be reborn in the plant or animal kingdoms. This was a development which ran parallel to the growing emphasis upon morality in the process. This is mainly ascribed to foreign influence upon Greek religion.(17) In general, the study of the Pythagorean doctrine is not of extreme importance to the present work because this philosophical school has been so far removed from the oldest beliefs concerning rebirth by learned speculation and foreign influences that it is only valuable in its role as an *interpretatio Graeca* to determine the *type* of belief that might be found among the Celts or Thracians. In fact, the religions of these more archaic Indo-European societies may be able to tell us more about the oldest stage of the Pythagorean system than it can tell us about the nature of these religious teachings.

India would also seem to provide us with an abundance of information on rebirth. However, when examining the Indian evidence we must restrict ourselves to the oldest period, and its literature, the hymns of the Ṛg Veda. The evidence provided there is at best inconclusive.(18) The type of texts generally found in the Ṛg Veda would not be conducive to such representations, and their language is poetic enough to be open to a variety of plausible interpretations.

In conclusion it must be said that there is no hard evidence to show that there was any common Indo-European ideology or belief in rebirth in this world, or "reincarnation." There have been scholars who have nevertheless postulated such a common belief paradigm for the Indo-European peoples.(19)

Non-Indo-European Traditions

The Finno-Ugric peoples, with their shamanistic form of religion, also developed a doctrine of rebirth. This teaching may well have been affected by, or have indeed affected, the Germanic and Indo-European version of this general belief. M. Eliade reports that according to the Yukagir tradition the psychic complex is composed of three components, or souls and that upon death each of these three entities fulfills a special function. One ascends to the sky, another remains with the corpse, and a third descends into a Kingdom of Shadows. This realm seems to reflect the nature of the earthly sphere. A shaman then descends into this Kingdom of Shadows in order to seek the soul and place it in the womb of a woman of his tribe, thus causing the rebirth of the soul. This process takes place within the family structure.(20)

Among many tribes of North American Indians similar beliefs may be found. These are especially interesting both because of their striking points of correspondence and because of the apparent lack of substantial cultural contact between these tribes and the Indo-European peoples.(21) The structure of the Amerindian soul is very much like that of the Germanic concept. Basically the psychic complex may be divided into five "souls":

I.   ego-soul
II . life-soul
III. breath-soul
IV.   free-soul
V.   guardian-soul ("power" and soul combined)

The first three entities are grouped together and referred to as "body-souls" which remain attached to the physical vehicle, and roughly represent consciousness, vital life manifestation, and a concentration of "life-stuff" respectively. The free-soul is considered to be manifested in dream, and to be manifested only outside the body. This free-soul is essentially an externalization of a passive body soul. On the other hand, the guardian-soul is active outside the body. It is the combination of "power" (e.g., *orenda, manitu*, etc.) and a free-soul into one conception.(22)

83

There are also a variety of well defined doctrines of rebirth among a number of North American tribes. A highly developed metaphysic is also provided by the soul conceptions presented above, which offer a definite framework for these teachings. The Hudson Bay Eskimos, and the Ingalik, Objibway, and Saulteaux Indian tribes believe in the reincarnation of the free-soul at the moment a child is given a name. They hold that the newborn baby will cry until the right name is pronounced over it, i.e., the name it had in its previous existence(s). The medicine men of the Carrier Indians catch the souls of the dead in their hands during the cremation rite and blow it into the body of another member of the tribe. The recipient of the soul then assumes the name of the dead person along side his own. Among the Yuchi Indians a child is named after a dead ancestor and the soul enters into the child.(23) These attestations also demonstrate the importance of either the clan or the tribe in the process of rebirth among the North American Indians. It is also interesting to note that the various souls were considered to have a variety of destinations after death: as ghosts wandering the earth, rebirth in a new body, or other-world existence, or perhaps gradual decay.(24) Regardless of the possibilities of cultural contact between the Germanic peoples and the pre-Columbian inhabitants of the far North American continent, the parallels in this matter are quite striking.

Footnotes to Chapter Six

1. E. Hull (1972), xxii ff.
2. In OIr. this "other-world" was known by a variety of names, e.g., Mag Már: "Great Plain', Mag Mell: "Happy Plain', Tír na mBan "Land of women', Tír na Finn: "Land of the Fair', Tír na nOc: "Land of Youth', Tír na mBeo: "Land of the (ever-)Living', Tír N-aill: "the other land', Tír Tall: "the next land', and Tír Tairngire "Land of Promise', which is probably based on the "Promised Land" of Hebraic mythology. These "lands" might have various "locations," e.g., to the west, under the sea, underground. Generally, however, this Celtic "other-world" is characterized by its constant interaction with "this-world," cf. for example the first branch of the *Mabinogion*.
3. J. de Vries (1961b), 250-258.
4. R. I. Best and O. Bergin (1929), 308.
5. Cf. the Tochmarc Etaine in R. I. Best and O. Bergin (1929) 207 ff.
6. K. Meyer (1882), 200.
7. R. I. Best and O. Bergin (1929), 334.
8. J. de Vries (1961b), 249-250, and (1956), I, 218.
9. M. Dillon and N. Chadwick (1967), 150.
10. Caesar *De Bello Gallico* VI, 14; Diodorus Siculus V, 28, 6, and III, 2; Strabo IV, 4, 4; Ammianus Marcellinus XV, 9; Lucanus Pharsalia I, 454-8, cf. J. de Vries (1961b), 248 ff.
11. T. D. Kendrik (1966), 108 ff, and J. de Vries (1961b), 250 ff.
12. K. Eckhardt (1937), 263 ff.
13. K. Eckhardt (1937), 103-104.
14. M. Eliade (1972), 22 ff.
15. E. Rohde (1925), 263.
16. Cf. E. Rohde (1925) for a thorough review of these various concepts.
17. K. Eckhardt (1937), 104 ff.
18. Vedic hymns which are often cited as evidence for "reincarnation" among the Vedic peoples are: *Ṛg Veda* I. 92.10, I. 164.32, I. 164.38, V. 46.1, X. 14.7-8, and X. 85.19.
19. K. Eckhardt (1937) and J. de Vries (1956 and 1961b) postulate an IE root system of rebirth ideology in which transmigration takes place within the tribe or family. Their evidence is chiefly Germanic, Celtic, Thracian, and Greek, and only secondarily Indo-Iranian. Their theories seem to work well in the western branch of IE culture, but do not entirely withstand the lack of ancient documentation.
20. M. Eliade (1964), 245.
21. Although it would not seem safe to assume any substantial contact between the IE cultures and that of the North American "Indians," it has been shown that the Germanic (Icelandic) contacts with North America occurred some five centuries before Columbus, and the possibility of even earlier European contacts have been raised. However, the vast Arctic culture may provide a more plausible link between the two in a religious context.

22. A. Hultkranz (1953), 149 ff.
23. A. Hultkranz (1953), 325 ff.
24. A. Hultkranz (1953), 477.

CHAPTER SEVEN

GERMANIC PARALLELS FOR SIGURÐR'S BOYHOOD "RITES OF TRANSFORMATION"

Rebirth (*aftrburðr*) in the Germanic world does not seem to be an automatic or instantaneous process, but rather there is a sequence of events, or rites, which usually follow the birth of a child and continue until he has "proven" that he is indeed the rebirth of his ancestor and worthy of the name which he was given at birth.(1) It seems necessary to discuss a selection of Germanic rites of transformation which deal in some way with *aftrburðr* and related doctrines. Non-Germanic parallels are also included by way of illustration. The importance or function of these motifs are extremely complex as they are found throughout Icelandic literature, and it is not suggested that these motifs should be interpreted exclusively according to the context in which they are found in the legend of Sigurðr. Here, the primary purpose is simply to demonstrate both the existence of these motifs outside the *Sigurðarsaga*. and their general importance within the socio-cultic and mythological spheres of the Germanic peoples.

Essentially, we are dealing with two phenomena: 1) parallelism of motifs, as they perhaps arise independently and are distributed in various narrative (or ritual) structures, and 2) thematic parallelism, that is, in the overall structure, or in the way in which these motifs are woven together. The former is quite common, while the latter is somewhat more difficult to find. This is not surprising considering the unitary nature of these mytho-ritualistic motifs which could be redistributed within various mythic or narrative structures.(2) Where those parallels in motif and theme fall together into an integrated whole, and in turn find a close thematic correspondence with the material in the story of Sigurðr, we most probably have an indicator of the mythic and cultural depth these characteristics must have enjoyed. The close thematic parallel between the Sigurðr-material and the 14th-century *Þórðar s. hr.* has already been mentioned, and will be discussed in even more detail later. Besides this late document, with apparently extremely archaic characteristics,(3) we may also detect similar traits in material of the *fornaldarsaga* type, as well as in mythological documents. Many heroes such as Sigmundr, Sinfjötli, Helgi, Starkaðr, and Hadingus have many motifs in common with the Sigurðr-mythos, i.e., rites of transformation, heroic education, vengeance, etc. However, none of these bear the same theme of the posthumous son who is the father reborn in order to avenge himself. This particular function (in heroic literature) has almost exclusively fallen together in the figure of Sigurðr Fáfnisbani. In the mythological materials we find this theme expressed to a certain degree by Víðarr in *ragnarök*. It is not exactly clear when Víðarr is born in relation to the death of Óðinn, but we are told that Víðarr is only three days old when he avenges his father.(4) This is hardly conclusive, but it does seem to indicate that Víðarr was engendered for this express purpose. The emphasis of this short but magically significant time period also seems to indicate the almost simultaneous nature of the death of Óðinn, and his rebirth and *hefnd*, or avenging, both through the figure of his son, Víðarr. This mythological necessity seems to be exemplified in the heroic realm by Sigurðr. Along with all the other gods to which the figure of Sigurðr has been linked, it seems that Víðarr must also be added to that list—as the *Vaterrachegott*. Indeed the Sigurðr-paradigm is sufficiently complex to find correspondences throughout the Germanic pantheon. He must, however, remain an essentially Óðinic figure.(5)

Before proceeding to the motif parallels, it seems advisable to say something concerning the most ancient cultural institutions which are reflected in these motifs.(6) The Germanic culture recorded by Tacitus and Caesar was different from that in which the story of Sigurðr was finally formulated and written down,(7) however, the institutions upon which these motifs were based had already been developed in an earlier time. Tacitus,(8) writing in 98 CE, describes a culture which believed itself to be descended from the primeval beings Tuisto and Mannus (*Germania* ch. 2) and which, at that time, worshiped Mercurius (= Óðinn) above all other gods (ch. 9). He also reports to some degree upon the initiatory institutions of the conferring of arms upon the warrior youth (ch. 13) in which the father, or some other relative (*vel propinqui*) presents the warrior with his weapons. The Germanic warriors of this period already showed the propensity to wander outside the tribal territory seeking battle and glory (ch. 14). The distribution of numinous and practical knowledge as well as battle wisdom is not within the province of Tacitus' text, however, he does allude to two points of knowledge given to Sigurðr. These are the wedge formation (phalanx) as a battle tactic (ch. 6) and the runes (in an early stage of development) which are perhaps indicated by the word *notae* in connection with divinatory practices (ch. 10). The sword and the horse play prominent roles in both the martial and sacred aspects of life. The horse is mentioned by Caesar (55 BCE) in *De Bello Gallico*(9) (IV) as an important asset to the Germanic warrior. Tacitus reports on the sacred, divinatory aspects of the horse-cult in *Germania* (ch. 10),(10) and he also indicates their importance in war (ch. 6). According to Tacitus the horse also played an important role in the socio-cultic rituals of gift-giving (ch. 15), marriage (ch. 18), and inheritance (ch. 32). The horse, unlike other property, was not necessarily inherited by the oldest son, but rather it went to the most talented warrior among the sons. The sword is mentioned as a prominent weapon (ch. 6), and the giving of arms, as well as horses was considered an important custom (ch. 15). Prophecy and divination were weighty matters for the people of the *Germania* (ch. 10). It is also interesting to note the general importance of the uncle in this culture (ch. 20), this with regard to Sigurðr's *móðirbróðir*, Grípir. Caesar (IV), and Tacitus (ch. 21) both report on the practice of vengeance or vendetta, however, they also mention the acceptance of *wergeld*.(11) The ritualistic paradigm(12) of the first-kill exemplified by the *berserkr*-like warriors in ch. 31 of the *Germania* is noteworthy when viewed from the perspective of Sigurðr's vengeance and first-kill in the battle against the Hundingssynir.(13)

The following outline of parallels from Germanic and extra-Germanic Sources is arranged according to the eight elements of Sigurðr's early career. The material contained in each of the eight segments will be roughly arranged according to its qualitative proximity to the *Sigurðarasga*, Germanic mythic material first, with saga-literature following, then other Nordic and Germanic parallels. Extra-Germanic material is also included in last position.

O. Sigmundr's Death (The posthumous son)

The mythological material is inconclusive here, because the concepts of "death" and "time" are rather ambiguous. It is said that Váli avenges his brother, Baldr, when he is only one day old (Bd. 11), however, whether, at this point, his father, Óðinn, is "dead" or not, is not clear. It is hoped that Chapter VIII of this work will demonstrate a similar, but by no means identical, pattern for the *Sigurðarsaga* The importance of divine progenitorship has already been discussed in Chapter V. The idea of the posthumous son is well developed in the *fornaldarsögur*. The *Völsungasaga* itself provides a good example of this motif when Völsungr is born to Rerir's queen after his death (*VS* 2)(14) The birth of Sigurðr is of course the most prominent example of this motif. *Hrólfs s. kr.* contains the story of Agnarr, who is born after the killing of his father, and he quickly grows to a mighty hero (ch. 12).(15) The *KS* also know this motif. Óláfr Tryggvason is born after Tryggvi's killing, but the killers of Tryggvi are themselves killed soon after the death of the king. In ch. 4 of the 14th-century *Þórðar s. hr.* we find a most striking parallel, which has already been discussed above in connection with the doctrine of rebirth. The following sections will further demonstrate the importance of this motif in the case of Þórðr.

The scene of Hjördís coming to Sigmundr as the hero lay dying on the battlefield is paralleled in the HHj 39-43, in which Sváva comes to the dying Helgi, and it is stated that both were reborn as Helgi Hundingsbani and Sigrún.

With the extra-Nordic realm, the story of Wolfram's *Parzivâl* bears a close resemblance to the posthumous son motif found in the story of Sigurðr. Gahmuret is killed in battle, and queen Herzeloyde gives birth to Parzival who grows to become a great knight. Finn mac Cumaill was also born under similar circumstances, as discussed above. The great heroes of the Celts and Greeks were most often considered the sons of the gods themselves. In such cases the "earthly" father is of little importance when compared to the role of the "celestial" father.(16)

I. Rites of Birth

These rites, which consist of the twofold ritual formula *verpa vatni á* (*vatni ausa*) and *gefa nafn* are attested in all types of Nordic literature from the mythic *Elder Edda* to the sagas representing later times with portrayals of the Christian baptism ritual, which replaced the older heathen custom. Instances of this procedure are so numerous that it seems necessary to cite only a selection of relevant passages here. In the *Elder Edda* we find two remarkable examples of the heathen ritual of *vatni ausa*. The Háv. 158 states:

Þat kann ec iþ þrettánda   ef ec scal þegn ungan
            verpa vanti á
munað hann falla   þótt hann í fólk momi,
       hníga sá halr fyr hiǫrom.

(That thirteenth I know   if I shall, upon a young warrior
            throw water
he will not fall   though he comes into battle,
       nor will that warrior fall before the sword.)

This runic stanza attributes the magical intent of invincibility to the rite. The "Rígsþula" (sts. 7, 21, and 34) describes each of the original representatives of the three social classes of Germanic society being "sprinkled with water" and being given their names.

In the cases of Starkaðr, Helgi Hjörvarþsson, and Helgi Hundingsbani (Sigmundarson) there is no mention of the rite of *vatni ausa*, however, the name-giving is of extreme importance in all three instances. The story of Starkaðr has already been discussed in Chapter V, where it was made clear that the name was an indication of the rebirth of the *jötunn* Starkaðr. The first Helgi was named by a *valkyrja*, Sváva, as he sat on a mound (haugr).(17) This *valkyrja* also gave him a sword as a name-gift.(18) Concerning. the second Helgi it is said that Sigmundr named his son after Helgi Hjörvarþsson. This is a secondary indication of the rebirth which is mentioned in the concluding prose of the HHj. Nornir came to Helgi Sigmundarson and " ... *þær er ǫðlingi aldr um scópo*" (...they [who] shaped the future life for the noble one).(19) In the *Völsungasaga* a similar story is told, and there King Sigmundr gives Helgi three name gifts: "Hringstaði ok Sólfjoll ok sverð" (Ring-place and Sun-mountain and a sword).(20) The Kings' Sagas and the Sagas of the Icelanders also abound with countless examples of these naming practices, where the formula usually appears: "*sá var vatni ausinn ok nafn gefit.*" Óláfr Tryggvason is named after Óláfr Geirstaðaálfr, as mentioned above.(21) The story of Þóðar Þórðarson continues to provide a parallel to the posthumous son-rebirth-avenging theme found in the story of Sigurðr In the *Þórðar s. hr.* (ch. 4) we read: "[*barnit*] *var vatni ausit ok nafn gefit, ok skyldi heita Þórðr eptir feðr sínum.*" The Anglo-Saxons also had a tradition which combined the rites of name-giving and sprinkling with water.(22)

91

Outside the Germanic realm one is struck by the similarity in function between the dipping of Achilles in the river Styx and the magical formula found in the "Hávamál" above. It is also interesting to note the functional parallel between the Germanic *vatni ausa* and the baptism of Culhwch in the story of Culhwch and Olwen in the *Mabinogion*.(23) See Chapter VIII for an interpretation of this rite from a socio-cultic perspective.

II . Fosterage

The heroic scenarios of the *Elder Edda* and the *fornaldarsögur* invariably include fosterage, and often the hero goes to a dwarf, giant, or other *úmannlig* figure. In the prose introduction to the "Grímnismál" we read of Óðinn and Frigg fostering the two boys Agnarr and Geirröðr, during which time Óðinn advises his *fóstri* in the arts of shrewdness. Helgi Sigmundarson was fostered to Hagall (the Skillful),(24) Hadingus was fostered to the two giants Vagnhofde and Hafte, and Starkaðr was fostered to a hypostasis of Óðinn called Hrosshárgrani. In other Germanic traditions it is told that Þiðrekr was fostered to Hilldebrandr (*ÞS* ch. 15). In the "Velentssaga" (found in the *ÞS*) we read that Velent (ON: Völundr) is first fostered to the smith Mímir, during the time of Sigurðr's fosterage (*ÞS* ch. 57). Later (*ÞS* ch. 58) Velent is fostered to the dwarves of Kallava, who taught him more of the smith's craft. In Germanic tradition the role of foster-father or foster-mother usually signified inferiority on the part of the foster parent. Also the foster-child was not particularly responsible to take blood vengeance for the death of a foster-parent.(25) Both of these points may further elucidate the nature of the relationship between Sigurðr and Reginn. Although the institution of fosterage is less prominent in the *KS* and *IS* it still plays an important role.(26)

Extra-Germanic sources also abound with examples of fosterage. In the Celtic realm the stories of Cú Chulainn and Finn are most remarkable. Cú Chulainn, the son of the god Lug, is fostered to the court of King Conchobar, where he plays havoc with the boy-corps.(27) Cú Chulainn later goes to Scathach and "fosters" himself to her in order to learn skill-at-arms.(28) A similar situation is the case with Finn mac Cumaill. When he is born, he is secretly fostered to Fiacal mac Conchinn, Bodball the druidess and the Gray One of Luachar. Bodball and the Gray One took him to the forest of Sliab Bladma and secretly reared him there.(29)

The heroic mythology of the Greeks also contains the fosterage motif. There we often find that the heroes are fostered to, and educated by, the centaur, Chiron.(30) This is the case with Achilles, Aeneas, Asclepios, Jason, Peleos and Polyxenus.(31)

III. Education

The education of the hero may be carried out in several different fields, by several different teachers. In this phase of the Sigurðr-material we find that Reginn teaches Sigurðr the kingly arts: runic lore (reading and writing of runes), playing *tafl*, and the speaking of many languages, besides the lore of Andvari's hoard. Later Óðinn himself teaches Sigurðr the tactics of warfare and other warrior-wisdom. Outside Germanic tradition we also find this "education of the hero" to be a popular theme. As mentioned above, both Cú Chulainn and Finn were taught skill-at-arms by warrior-women. The Greek heroes also had their 'mentors' who would teach them skills and knowledge.

IV. Reception of the Horse

This motif is not very amply developed in the oldest Germanic literature, however, the general importance of the horse in both the secular and the sacred realms cannot be denied.(32) It seems that the horse was an important gift which one person might give to another.(33) In the version of the legend of Sigurðr found in the *Þiðreks saga*, Sigurðr does not receive Grani until the meeting with Brynhildr, where he is ceremoniously presented with horse, sword, and gold, in a medieval style reminiscent of the *Schwertleite* ceremony (*ÞS* ch. 168). The horse, or some reference to it always seems to insert itself in some way into the story of a hero. In the story of Starkaðr we notice that Óðinn's *heiti* is Hrosshárgrani, and in the Hadingus-legend it is upon a horse (Sleipnir) that Óðinn takes the hero away in order to foretell his future. The horse is often connected to ideas of death, or passage from one state of being to another.(34) Symbolically, men and horses are very closely connected.(35) In Chapter VIII of this work we will further develop the possible significance of the horse, and of the way in which Sigurðr receives Grani from Óðinn. The Norse mythic material about Sigurðr actually presents a relatively unique motif in this instance.

V. Reception of the Sword

The sword was an extremely important weapon and symbol in early Germanic society, and it is often considered to be sacred to either Týr or Freyr,(36) although most Óðinic heroes used the sword as their primary weapon. In the *CR*, it is with the sword that Víðarr is said to avenge his father's death.(37) Here, we are principally interested in the transmission, or inheritance of the sword. The inheritance of the hammer, Mjöllnir, by Magni and Móði reminds us of the motif found so often in saga literature where the child inherits the weapon(s) of the father or some other ancestor. Archeological evidence also indicates that weapons were very often handed down from generation to generation for hundreds of years.(38)

In the *CR* we find that Helgi Hjörvarþsson is given his name by a *valkyrja* and with that name she also gives a sword.(39) In this, as well as many other cases, it seems significant that the sword is given to the hero by a female (sometimes maternal) figure. The *Flb.* relates the story of Óláfr inn helgi, which has already been touched upon. In this saga we learn that after Hrani has seen to the birth of the son of Haraldr and Ásta, he names the child Óláfr, and gives him the sword, Bæsing, as a *nafnfestr* (name-gift).(40) The sagas of Víga-Glumr and Hallfreðr also provide interesting parallels in that in both cases the sword is closely connected with the *hamingja* or *ættarfylgja*, and the transference of that entity.(41) It is also interesting to note the manner in which the older Hallfreðr obtained the sword, Konungsnautr. As its name indicates, it was a gift to Hallfreðr from King Óláfr Tryggvason. When Óláfr gave Hallfreðr the nickname "*vandræðaskáld*" the skald asked for and received the sword as a *nafnfestr*.(42)

The Norse myth of Sigurðr provides us with one of the most powerful examples of the inheritance or transfer of ownership of a *sigrsverð*, or "victorious sword." The god, Óðinn, plunges the sword, Gramr, deep into the "apple"-tree, called Barnstokkr. Only Sigmundr is able to pull the sword out, and thus he inherits the sword, and its power.(43) This would seem to amount to the god giving the gift of *hamingja* to himself, in view of the true nature of the hero, Sigmundr.(44) This could also be interpreted as a mythic representation of a ritual, which is later reflected in the *Hirðskrá* as the *sverðtaka*. In this ceremony the *þegn* takes a sword from the *konungr* and thus becomes his *sverðtakari*, his "sword-taker."(45) The sword is a token, a talisman, which bears the *hamingja* of the king. This general principle is at the root of most traditions surrounding the wondrous swords of Germanic legend. The *fylgja*, or *hamingja* of an entire clan (*ættarfylgja*) may be embodied in the sword.(46)

The following examples are not only important because they seem to indicate a clear tradition of clanic inheritance of the *hamingja* (and more especially the *ættarfylgja*), but also because they show the reception of this talisman of power *from the mother* of the hero. In the saga of Böðvarr Bjarki we read that Böðvarr is advised by his mother to go to a cave in order to retrieve the weapons his father had hidden just before his death. When Böðvarr finds the sword he is able to pull it from a rock with ease.(47) Hervör, the posthumous daughter of Angantýr, takes his sword, Týrfing, from his *haugr* and does battle as a viking. Later, Hervör gives the sword to her son, Heiðrekr, who becomes as fierce as his grandfather.(48) In the *Grettissaga* we read that Grettir's mother, Ásdís, gives him the sword called Ættartangi (= the "hilt" of the clan), telling him: "*Sverð þetta átti Jökull, föðurfaðir minn, ok inir fyrri Vatnsdælar, ok var þeim sigrsælt. Vil ek nú gefa þér sverðit, ok njót vel*" (Jokull, my grandfather owned this sword, and the ancient Vatnsdæl-men, and it was victory-blessed for them. Now I want to give you the sword, and use it well).(49) The saga of Óláfr inn helgi continues to provide interesting material, when we read that the young Óláfr was in his mother's chamber one day and there he catches a glimpse of a sword in Ásta's chest. He asks her about it, and she replies that it is his name-gift. Then Ásta gives Óláfr the sword after telling him that it had once belonged to Óláfr Gerstaðaálfr.(50) In many of these legends (including that of Sigurðr) the sword is transferred from one male to another through a female. This method of transmission is perhaps a reflection of old initiatory patterns.(51)

This section of the **Sigurðarsaga* contains a secondary motif: the two *Schwertproben*. There are both Germanic and non-Germanic parallels for these. The cutting of the wool against the river current provides us with the best examples. In the *ÞS* (ch. 67) we read that Velent cuts a clump of felt against a stream in order to test the keenness of his work, the sword Mímung. Cú Chulainn's sword is said to be so sharp that it can cut hair against the stream.(52) Celtic tradition knows well the importance of taking up arms for the first time. Cú Chulainn must have the finest possible weapons, those of King Conchobar, in order to fight properly.(53) Later, Cú Chulainn receives his most prized weapon, the *gae bulga*, or "bag-spear," from his mentor-at-arms, Scathach.(54) In Greek mythology the story of Theseus recovering the sword and shoes from under a rock where his father had placed them, is somewhat similar to the Sigmundr motif.(55)

VI. Prophecy

The foretelling of the future of a hero often plays an important part in his development. This act may be considered to be as much magical (operative) as divinatory. That is, the prophet may be as much an active agent in the formation of the future as he is a passive transmitter.(56) In the case of Helgi Sigmundarson, as well as of many others, this prophetic episode took place upon his birth, when *nornir* came to him and foretold his future greatness.(57) Starkaðr receives the blessings of Óðinn and the curses of Þórr, which act as a foretelling of his entire life.(58) Óðinn tells Hadingus about his future captivity, battle with the lion, subsequent acquisition of superhuman strength, and ultimate escape.(59)

Outside Germanic lore we also find ample evidence for a tradition of prophecy as an important stage in a heroic career. The future of Cú Chulainn was foretold on at least three different occasions, by three different soothsayers. The druid, Cathbad, with his prophecy, at once foretold Cú Chulainn's greatness and was the agent of Cú Chulainn's desire to become a great hero.(60) Later the youth Eochaid Bairche gives Cú Chulainn a prophecy, and also Scathach delivers an oracle to the hero while he is with her learning skill-at-arms. It is not clear how much of this tradition springs from cultic practices of divination (performed at births, and upon important occasions, etc.) and how much is later literary technique.

VII. Vengeance

The close connection between blood-vengeance and rebirth has already been briefly touched upon in Chapter V above. Vengeance was an ethically binding responsibility, which was not dependent upon filial love. This is probably the single most prevalent theme in all of old Germanic literature, and therefore the examples are numerous. The most important parallel examples for our study are those of Víðarr and Váli, the Helgar Sigmundr and Turf-Einarr. Víðarr avenges his father and is "reborn" in the post-*ragnarök* world, Váli avenges his brother, Baldr, and is also reborn. It is even possible that Váli is in fact Baldr reborn.(61) Helgi Hjörvarþsson avenges his *móðirfaðir*. The saga of the Völsungs is full of deeds of vengeance. Rerir avenges his father, Sigi. Sigmundr, with the help of Sinfjötli, his son, avenges Völsungr, while in the *CR* (HHII) Helgi Sigmundarson is said to avenge Sigmundr on Hundingr. The *Heimskringla* records an important instance of *Vaterrache* by an Óðinic hero. Turf-Einarr, who is one-eyed, avenges the death of his father by carving the *blóðgar örn*, or "bloody eagle," on Hálfdan hlálegg.(62) This was evidently a typical form of Óðinic sacrifice.

The *Þórðar s. hr.* again provides a perfect parallel in this regard. Þórðr (II) sets out and avenges his father on Bárekr, and afterward "... *þótti hann mikit hafa vaxit af verki þessu*" (he was thought to have grown great by this deed).(63)

Footnotes to Chapter Seven

1. See the conclusion of Ch. IV for an outline of the structure of these motifs as they are present in the *Sigurðarsaga*.
2. See P. Buchholz (1977), and L. Motz (1973b).
3. See M. Keil (1931), 79; 91 concerning the archaic nature of this saga.
4. Cf. also that Váli is only one day old when he avenges Baldr and Magni is only three days old when he lifts the leg of Hrugnir from his father.
5. This association is aided by Óðinn's apparent omnipresence throughout the Gmc. pantheon.
6. Our evidence for these cultural institutions is provided mainly by classical ethnographers and historians.
7. The two particular cultures in question are separated by a millennium and the North Sea, and therefore this is not surprising, however the correspondences between the two cultures remain quite remarkable.
8. The edition of Tacitus used here is that of R. Much (1937).
9. The edition of *De Bello Gallico* used here is that of Fr. Kraner and W. Dittenberger (1961).
10. Cf. R. Much (1937), 135 ff. See also Ch. VIII.
11. For a review of the legal aspects of wergeld in the context of birth and rebirth, cf. K. Eckhardt (1937), 87-89.
12. This would be a negative, dynamistic rite as analyzed according to A. van Gennep.
13. See Ch. VIII, especially the discussion of *hefna*.
14. Völsungr appears to be more the direct son of Óðinn rather than of Rerir. This portion of the *VS* is probably somewhat later than the material of the Völsungr-Sigmundr-Sigurðr legends.
15. See this chapter for a discussion of Agnarr's revenge.
16. The "other-world" father. For a study of the psychological function of the archetypal father in the hero myth, see E. Neumann (1954), 170-191.
17. See H. R. Davidson (1943), 105 ff. for a discussion of this custom.
18. See HHj., the prose introducing section II, sts. 6-9, and the following prose.
19. See HHI st. 2.
20. Here, Helgi may be contrasted with Sigurðr in that the latter hero won his fame without benefit of such name-gifts. Sigurðr possessed the necessary innate *hamingja*, but had to prove himself gradually in order to attain the gifts symbolic of these types of power (royal, numinous, and martial).
21. For a collection of examples from the *ÍS* and *KS*, cf. K. Eckhardt (1937), 74 ff. It is also probable that the form and function of the Christian baptismal rite, as it is found in the Gmc. territories was actually heavily influenced by the heathen formulas. Cf. K. Müllenhoff (1881) in response to Maurer (1881).
22. K. Eckhardt (1937), 77 and O. Schrader (1901) 557 ff.

23. G. Jones and T. Jones (1974), 95. It is probable that this is a Christian interpolation into an essentially pagan structure.

24. Cf. HHII beginning prose, Hagall (= the skillful) is probably a dwarf.

25. S. Barlau (1975), 134 ff.

26. For numerous examples of fosterage in various cultural contexts cf. S. Barlau (1975).

27. This is reminiscent of the way Sigurðr treats the apprentices in Mímir's smithy in the ÞS.

28. T. Cross and C. Slover (1936), 162-168.

29. T. Cross and C. Slover (1936), 361-362.

30. Note the fosterage to a non-human (chthonic) being, as a parallel to the Gmc. situation with respect to dwarves and giants.

31. J. de Vries (1963), 214

32. See references to passages in Tacitus and Caesar above, and also cf. the general importance of the horse in IE culture and religion.

33. R. Cleasby and G. Vigfusson (1957), 260.

34. Cf. the name Yggdrasill (the World Tree): "Ygg's (= Óðinn's) steed," especially in connection with Óðinn's runic initiation described in Háv. sts. 138-141, and the general importance of the horse in the shamanistic tradition of northern Eurasia; cf. M. Eliade (1964), 151; 217; 173 ff; and 466 ff.

35. Cf. the riddle in the *Heiðreks saga*, st. 72:

Hverir eru þeir tveir	Who are those two
er tíu hafa fœtr	who have ten feet
augu þrjú	three eyes
ok einn hala?	and one tail?
(= Óðinn riding Sleipnir)	

It is also perhaps worth noting in this regard that in the Older Futhark the runes for "horse" (*ehwaz*) M (19) and "man" (*mannaz*) Ħ (20) are placed next to one another, and that their shapes perhaps reveal a further intended connection.

36. As related in the "Lokasenna" st. 42, Freyr gave up his sword as a bridal gift to the giant Gymir for his daughter, Gerðr. The sword as a bridal gift is mentioned in *Germania* (ch. 18), and is more fully discussed by H. R. Davidson (1960), 2 ff. The sword seems to have passed into the domain of Óðinn in the later period, perhaps indicated, or aided by the myth of Freyr giving his sword away.

37. Vsp. st. 53 indicates Víðarr uses a sword to avenge Óðinn.

38. Cf. H. R. Davidson (1960), 5 ff., and H. Falk (1914), 39 ff.

39. HHj. sts. 6-9.

40. *Flb.* I, ch. 7.

41. *Hallfreðar saga*, ch. 11.

42. *Hallfreðar saga*, ch. 6.

43. *VS* ch. 3. This is of course somewhat paralleled by the Arthurian legend of Excalibur; see Ch. VIII.

44. The name "Sigmundr" is considered an *Óðinsheiti*, H. Falk (1924), 25.

45. Cf. R. Cleasby and G. Vigfusson (1957), 610, and the Hirðskrá (the book of laws pertaining to the king's retainers).

46. H. R. Davidson (1960) , 9 ff., and V. Grönbech (1931), II, 27 ff.

47. *Hrólfs s. kr.*, ch. 31.

48. *Hervarar saga*, chs. 4-5.

49. *Grettis saga*, ch. 17 .

50. *Flb.*, II, ch. 12.

51. The transmission of numinous knowledge in this manner is well known and amply attested in the *CR*, e.g., the recovery of the poetic mead by Óðinn from Gunnlöð (Háv. sts. 104-110), and also Háv. st. 164 in which this type of initiation is perhaps reflected. The the Sigurðr-material itself contains an example of this. In the "Sigdrífumál" we find Sigurðr receiving runic wisdom from the *valkyrja* Sigrdrífa. There are many other examples from the sagas, and almost all of them have strong sexual implications. Celtic tradition also maintains similar practices, cf. Cú Chulainn and Scathach.

52. T. Cross and C. Slover (1936), 313.

53. T. Cross and C. Slover (1936) , 143.

54. T. Cross and C. Slover (1936) , 168.

55. R. A. Hendricks (1972), 170.

56. W. R. Halliday (1913), 53.

57. *VS*, ch. 8.

58. *Gautreks saga*, ch. 7.

59. Saxo, Book I.

60. T. Cross and C. Slover (1936), 142 ff; 164; 165-168.

61. J. de Vries (1955), 56.

62. *Haralds saga hárfagra*, ch. 31.

63. *Þórðar s. hr.*, ch. 4.

CHAPTER EIGHT

INTERPRETATIONS AND COMMENTARY
ON THE *SIGURÐARSAGA

Research presented in the foregoing chapters was intended to act as a cosmological, mythic, or traditional framework for the interpretation ventured here. Moreover, it is hoped that the commentaries presented in this chapter will, to some degree, elucidate the mythological, psycho-magical, and socio-cultic(1) processes which seem to be active in this segment of the legends of Sigurðr. This study is of course primarily concerned with the ideology of *aftrburðr*, and how it was supported by the tradition, metaphysic, and cult of Germanic religion in the late heathen period. However, in order to examine this doctrine thoroughly, these three aspects must be kept in mind. The following interpretive commentaries attempt, as much as possible, to remain confined to the religious psychology and phenomenology of the late heathen age, already largely outlined in chapters V and VII above, without resort to modern psychological interpretation.

This chapter is arranged in three main sections. The first of these is a discussion of the textual and thematic evidence which indicate that Sigurðr is Sigmundr "*aptrborinn*." An interpretation of this process with regard to the pertinent section of the story of Sigurðr follows in the section entitled <u>Sigmundr's Death</u>. This discussion is focused upon the textual passages concerning the death of Sigmundr and the moment of Sigurðr's birth. The third section deals with the various rites and religio-ethical institutions portrayed and/or reflected in this segment of the *Sigurðarsaga*. which seem to facilitate the process of *aptrburðr*. Many of these institutions also served as more general *Stationen des Heldenlebens* in the heroic rites of transformation. However, the commentary presented in this section is primarily interested in these rites as institutions supporting the ideology of *aftrburðr*, and only secondarily concerned with the broader socio-cultic implications. This is done with full knowledge that these two functions are by no means mutually exclusive, but on the contrary, are closely interwoven with one another. For purposes of this study, however, the distinction has been drawn between the function of these rites purely as facilitators of *aftrburðr* in the Sigurðr-myth, and their broader initiatory functions, which tended to continue even after belief in *aftrburðr* had begun to wane.

In all of these sections an attempt has been made to adhere to both the actual texts of the *CR-VS* version of the Sigurðr's story and to the schematic analysis of those texts with regard to the *aptrburðr* theme presented at the conclusion of Chapter IV. It must be emphasized that the interpretation is by no means a complete commentary upon the importance of this section of the Sigurðr-material. When dealing with mythic material, such as that with which we are confronted in these texts, it seems that no single approach may be entirely satisfactory. Myth, as with all other living systems is far too complex to be reduced to one rule or formulaic approach. A thorough study of all the initiatory rites of transformation present in the Sigurðr-myth would greatly expand our understanding of these important texts.

Internal Evidence for the *Aptrburðr* of Sigmundr

In order to examine the evidence internal to the *CR-VS* version we must extend our view beyond the segment of the legend of Sigurðr in question here, back to the story of Sinfjötli and forward to the slaying of Fáfnir. Within those two passages in both the *VS* and *CR*, we find pieces of evidence, which, when juxtaposed, convincingly demonstrate the rebirth aspect. This evidence must be viewed within the context of Germanic mythology and culture. In the *VS* ch. 10 and in the prose section of the *CR* called "*Frá dauða Sinfjötla*" we read how both Sigmundr and Sinfjötli drink a poisoned draught—but only Sinfjötli dies, because as we read in the *CR*: "*Svá er sagt at Sigmundr var harðgǫrr, at hvárki mátti hánom eitr granda útan né innan; en allir synir hans stóðozk eitr á hǫrund útan*" (Thus it is said that Sigmundr was so hardy, that poison could harm him neither on the outside nor on the inside; but all of his sons could stand it on their skin outside). [Sf. 12-15] While the *VS* says in ch. 7: "*Sigmundr var svá mikill fyrir sér, at hann mátti eta eitr, svá at hann skaðaði ekki, en Sinfjötla hlýddi þat, at eitr kæmi útan á hann, en eigi hlýddi honum at eta þat né drekka*" (Sigmundr was so powerful [in himself] that he could eat poison, so that it would do him no harm, but Sinfjötli could stand it, that poison could come onto him on the outside, but he could not stand to eat it nor drink [it]). We also find the following passage in ch. 52 of the *ESS* (*Skáldskaparmál*): "*Svá er sagt, at Sigmundr Vavlsvngsson var svá mattvgr, at hann drack eitr ok sakaþi ecki, en Sinfiotli sonr hans ok Sigurðr voro svá harþir, ahvona, at þá sakaþi ecki eitr, at vtan qvæmi*" (Thus it is said, that Sigmundr Völsungarson was so mighty

102

that he drank poison and it did not harm him, but Sinfjötli his son and Siguròr so hard on their skins that poison could not harm them, that might come from the outside). Here, the key is the idea that all of Sigmundr's sons could stand poison on their skins, but only Sigmundr himself could actually ingest it and live. The passage from the *ESS* could have possibly added Siguròr beside Sinfjötli because Siguròr was also known to be one of his sons. However, if the conclusions reached in this chapter are correct, Siguròr too had the ability to ingest poison.

Now, when we examine the evidence in the *VS* chs. 18-20, and the first prose section and the prose sections following sts. 31 and 39 of the "Fáfnismál," we find that the poisonous blood (*sveiti*) of the worm-giant Fáfnir does indeed touch him on the skin: "... *ok hefir allar hendr blóðgar upp til axlar*" (... and his arms are all bloody up to the shoulders) [VS ch. 18].(2) In the first prose section of the "Fáfnismál" we read: "... blés hann (Fáfnir) eitri ok hraut fyrir ofan hǫfuð Siguròri" (... he [Fáfnir] blew poison and it fell from above onto Siguròr's head).

Here, we must pause in order to establish that the substance referred to variously as *blóð* and *sveiti* are indeed identical, and that they both constitute *eitr* in this context. In *VS* ch. 18 it is made explicit that the word *sveiti*: "sweat" is equivalent to *blóð*: "blood." For example, Siguròr asks Reginn: "*Hversu mun þá veita ef ek verð fyrir sveita ormsins?*" (What will happen then if I get in front of the blood of the serpent?). This is asked after Reginn tells Siguròr to dig a ditch and stab Fáfnir as he crawls over it. Later in the same chapter Óðinn advises Siguròr differently when he says: "Ger fleiri grafar ok lát þar í renna sveitann" (Dig more ditches and let the blood run in there). It is not completely clear why Óðinn advised this, and it is not the purpose of this study to provide that explanation. However, it does seem rather clear that Óðinn is not particularly trying to keep the *eitr* from running onto the hero, but rather he might have other plans for the blood, and it is better to store the blood rather than use it directly.(3) There are several other examples of Germanic heroes who do have to protect themselves from the poison spewed forth by serpents.(4) Dictionaries gloss Old Norse *sveiti* with both "blood" and "sweat," and the association seems quite archaic.(5) Besides this evidence for the identity of "blood" and "sweat," and their poisonous nature with reference to Fáfnir in the *Völsungasaga*, there also exists a wealth of evidence in *Bēowulf* concerning the poisonous, corrosive

103

nature of the blood of monstrous (*úmannlig*) creatures. When Bēowulf strikes off the head of Grendel, the blood (OE *swāt*) of the creature causes the sword to melt.(6) Two other passages in *Bēowulf* refer specifically to the corrosive nature of serpents' blood.(7) Thus, it seems rather clear that with respect to monstrous creatures in general, and Fáfnir in particular, we are dealing with a being which possesses a venomous type of blood.

In three texts (*VS*, *CR*, and *ESS*) we learn that Sigurðr ingests some of this poisonous blood of the worm, and it does him no harm. Quite to the contrary, the blood causes him to understand the "language of the birds," i.e., he receives special psychic powers.(8) This occurs when Sigurðr is roasting the heart of Fáfnir so that his *fóstri*, Reginn, might eat it. During this, he touches the bloody, bubbling heart in order to test it, and in the process burns his finger. Instinctively, he puts his finger into his mouth, *"En er hiartblóð Fáfnis kom á tungo hanom—ok skilði hann fuglsrǫdd"* (But when the heart-blood of Fáfnir came onto his tongue—he could also understand the bird-speech). ["Fáfnismál" prose after st. 34](9) Also in the "Fáfnismál," after Sigurðr has learned of Reginn's treachery by means of the *fuglsrödd*, we find a passage which reads: *"Sigurðr hió hǫfuð af Regin, ok þá át hann Fáfnis hiarta ok drakk blóð þeira beggia, Regins ok Fáfnis"* (Sigurðr hewed the head off of Reginn and then he ate Fáfnir's heart and drank the blood of them both, of Reginn and of Fáfnir). ["Fáfnismál" prose after st. 39] These passages demonstrate that not only is Sigurðr invulnerable to the venom, but that the blood of members of an *úmannlig ætt*—a non-human type of being—which is normally poisonous to humans, only brings him more power and numinous knowledge. From this evidence it would seem correct to conclude that indeed Sigurðr is not merely the son of Sigmundr, but rather he *is* Sigmundr reborn—at least with regard to certain powers embodied in the *hamingja-fylgja* of the elder hero.(10)

Besides this internal, textual evidence, there also exists some thematic and comparative evidence drawn from other Old Norse documentation, which involves naming practices and rebirth.(11) As has already been pointed out, the theme-variation naming system was an alternate form of *Nachbenennung*, and both systems seem to be equally indicative of a belief in *aftrburðr*. The fact that the names of the two heroes in question here are related in just this way (Sigmundr : Sig-urðr), coupled with the motif of the posthumous son, would probably lead contemporary audiences of the *Sigurðarsaga* to the conclusion that Sigurðr *was* Sigmundr "*aptrborinn.*" The name "Sig-mundr" is usually analyzed as a compound of *sig-*: "victory" and *mundr*: "gift" or "dowry' while "Sig-urðr" may be analyzed as a compound of *sig-*: "victory" and *vörðr*: "warder" '(< *SigiwarðuR) —or a folk etymology connecting the second half of the compound name with the name for the first of the Nornir, Urðr, may also play some role in the special reception of the name among the west Norse peoples. Beyond this naming motif, certain thematic features and many motifs within this phase of the story of Sigurðr are found elsewhere in Old Norse literature. In many of these cases the question of rebirth is more easily discernible because of the extreme simplicity of the narrative. The *Þórðar saga hreðu*(12) (*Þórðar s. hr.*) is one such document which is devoid of the manifold complications of the *Sigurðarsaga*, and one in which the rebirth theme present in the the the Völsung material is perfectly paralleled in its most essential points. The general sequence of events in the *Þórðar s. hr.* and its overt rebirth theme have already been outlined in Chapter VII of the present work, but a short schematic presentation may make the close parallel even more obvious:

Sigurðarsaga (VS-CR)	*Þórðar s. hr.*
I. Sig-mundr killed	Þórðr (1) killed
II. Sigurðr born (posthumously)	Þórðr (2) born (posthumously)
III. Named "after" father	Named after father
IV. Protected and nurtured by mother, and educated by *fóstri.*	Protected and nurtured by mother
V. Avenges father at a young age	Avenges father at age twelve

This scheme forms an important part of the process of interpretation presented in this chapter, especially with regard to the naming practice and the function of vengeance in the Nordic religio-ethic.

Sigmundr's Death

Textually, the following commentaries and interpretations are principally concerned with the *Völsungasaga* passages in chs. 11, 12 and the first sentence of ch. 13, all of which deal with the death of

105

Sigmundr and the birth of Sigurðr. This passage contains an abundance of material which is meaningful in the mythological, psycho-magical, as well as socio-cultic realms. The role of Óðinn is of primary importance in the mythological considerations, however, Hjördís is also noteworthy in this regard. The psycho-magical realm is emphasized by both the probable psychic phenomena involved with the "dying man," and the general concept of the *dís*. While the socio-cultic characteristics surface in the death scene itself as well as the *sverðgipt* episode which also deserves some comment in this context.

It is well known from the sagas that although Óðinn aids his heroes, he is also usually instrumental in their downfalls. This situation was even noted, and commented upon by the skaldic poets of the 10th-century. In the "Eiríksmál" st. 7, we read:

Hví namt hann sigri þá	Why did you take victory from him
es þér þótti snjallr vesa?(13)	if it seemed to you he was valiant?
Óvist's at vita,	It is unknown to know,
sér úlfr enn hǫsvi	the gray wolf looks
[greypr] á sjǫt goða.(14)	grimly at the gods' dwelling.

This st., as well as the "Hákonarmál" sts. 10 ff., and several other passages in Icelandic literature,(15) explain that Óðinn causes the death of great and heroic kings, that he may bring them into *Valhöll*, thus swelling the ranks of the *einherjar*, which will fight alongside the gods at *ragnarök*.(16) The paradoxical aspects of Óðinn's behavior are also well within his essentially unified and ever-expanding mythological function.(17)

In order to understand the importance of Sigmundr's death more completely we must examine his origins more carefully. Sigmundr is the direct descendant of Óðinn. The *Völsungaætt* begins with Sigi, a son of Óðinn. The clan is subsequently revivified by the Óðinic *hamingja* when the wife of Rerir Sigason is impregnated with the aid of an apple sent from Óðinn to Rerir.(18) The name of their son, Völsungr, becomes the patronym of the clan, and the name seems to imply that it is Óðinn in his aspect as Völsi, who is actually the divine father of Völsungr.(19) King Völsungr in turn engenders Sigmundr. However, even in this case Óðinn again takes a direct hand in increasing his power and influence over the development of the *Völsungaætt*. This is of course affected by the famous *sverðgipt* episode portrayed in *Völsungasaga* ch. 3. Here, Óðinn enters the hall of King Vösungr during a wedding feast. This hall is built in such a way that a great *apaldr* (= "apple," or generally fruit-bearing tree) stood in its center so that its branches spread out over the roof and the trunk descended down into the hall. This tree was called *barnstokkr* (= child, or birth-trunk), and is not only analogous to Yggdrasill, but also an important fertility symbol. Óðinn then plunges a sword into the trunk of this tree and declares: "*Sá er þessu sverði bregðr ór stokkinum, þá skal sá þat þiggja at mér at gjöf, ok skal hann sjálfr sanna at aldri bar hann betra sverð sér í hendi e[n þetta er].*" (He who draws this sword from the trunk, then he shall receive it from me as a gift, and he shall himself affirm that he never bore a better sword in his hand than this is.) Several men in the hall attempt to pull it out—to no avail. Then Sigmundr approached, gripped the sword, "*... ok var sem laust lægi fyrir honum*" (... and it was as if it had lain loose before him). Thus it is clear that this episode does not represent a test-of-strength, but rather an initiatory election.(20)

The two symbols which are prominent in this scene are the tree and the sword. The tree can be understood as a symbol for the center of the cosmos,(21) and a strong fertility symbol. The scene in general may be reminiscent of certain temple structures of the ancient North which symbolized the cosmos. J. de Vries connects the sword with the spear—the most ancient symbol of Germanic royal power.(22) The ritual of *sverðtaka* may also be reflected in this passage.(23) In any event, the sword is a bearer of *hamingja* which attaches itself to its recipient. The idea that the *hamingjur*, *fylgjur*, or *valkyrjur* would attach themselves to swords is well attested in Icelandic literature,(24) and these passages are discussed in Chapter V and below in Chapter VIII of this work. Moreover, the tree-sword complex is an extremely important fertility symbol, and in this case one of cosmic fertility.(25) Certain trees were considered bearers of *hamingja*.(26) This *sverðgipt* episode may be interpreted safely as a transference of *hamingja* from Óðinn to Sigmundr. While the structure of the events described seems to draw upon a blend of marriage-fertility ceremonial and culto-martial ritual.

When Óðinn comes onto the field of battle, where Sigmundr is in combat with King Siggeirr, and breaks the sword in two with his spear, more than just a sword is broken. It is said that Sigmundr's 'luck' turned from him ("*Sigmundi horfinn heill*") [VS ch. 3]. As a result of Óðinn's intervention Sigmundr falls in the fight, mortally wounded. The motives of the god seem clear, especially when understood within the *aftrburðr* context: Óðinn fathers clans of great heroes, develops each of them to their ultimate potential, then takes them into *Valhöll*—while their (his) *hamingja* is reborn to be even more powerfully developed through heroic action in subsequent births. By this method he may stock the *einherjar* with ever greater heroes. Óðinn sows, cultivates, and harvests his seed, but always returns a portion of it to the earth to insure even greater qualitative harvests in the future. Also, in this instance the broken sword must be understood as a kind of "deactivated" *hamingja*, but one which gathers power in its nine months of slumber.

Before returning to the symbolism of the broken sword in this rebirth theme, we must more carefully examine Sigmundr's death itself for evidence of a possible *aftrburðr* related motif. As Sigmundr lay dying he tells Hjördís, who has come to him on the battlefield, that she is pregnant with a son. He then delivers a prophecy concerning the future greatness of this hero. The function of this prophecy can best be understood within the context of certain metaphysical concepts surrounding "the dying man."(27) As a man is dying, and the *hugr* is being released, the person comes into momentary contact with the realm of the dead, and he becomes conscious of certain hidden future events or occult wisdom which he is then able to tell. This also seems to be the fundamental concept behind Óðinn's initiation described in Háv. sts. 138-141, although in that instance the god (initiate) survives the death experience and returns to the realm of the living with numinous knowledge.(28) Besides this essentially passive, mystical function of prophecy, it is also quite possible that Sigmundr is actually able to project an aspect of the soul (*hamingja-fylgja*) into the womb of Hjördís, thus helping to assure his *aftrburðr* in a magical way. The willed directing of the *hamingja-fylgja* has already been noted in Chapter V. The function of the female, in this case, Hjördís, is of extreme importance.

It is at this stage that the function of the broken sword, or dormant *hamingja*, must again be considered. Sigmundr entrusts the pieces of the sword to Hjördís, telling her to have them re-forged for the son she will bear so that he may avenge Sigmundr and Eylimi. Here, Sigmundr not only entrusts a sword to the care of Hjördís, but he is also commending the *hamingja* which is attached to it. Thus, this is a parallel action to his prophecy which constitutes a type of rite of separation, i.e., the *hamingja* is separated from the world of the living and begins a sojourn in the realm of the dead. It seems, in view of what is to come, that the prophecy and the entrusting of the sword represent the outward manifestations of two distinct processes, or rites of separation, which will require two distinct rites of reintegration. The prophecy projects the *mannsfylgja* while the sword is emblematic of of the *ættarfylgja*. Hjördís is the recipient of both of these entities. The motif of a female receiving and preserving a clanic heirloom weapon is not at all uncommon. This may be either a mother who keeps a weapon for her son, to give when he has demonstrated his maturity, or it may be held by a man's daughter and given as a part of a dowry.(29) The other famous instances of swords being preserved by mothers for their sons have been noted in Chapter VII above. In one of those examples (*Grettis saga*) we have a mother named Ásdís who keeps a family heirloom weapon for her son, Grettir. In the *Völsungasaga* we find a mother named Hjördís performing the same function. Here, it is the second element of the compound personal names (-dís) which interests us. The *dísir* as noted in Chapter V, are divine female beings, somewhat akin to the *fylgjur* and *valkyrjur* concepts. However, their more specific functions are involved with fertility and motherhood—and secondarily as wise-women and protective spirits.(30) There was a well developed cult of the *dísir*, and it is most probably that they were the souls of the female ancestors of the clan, but in any case the mysteries of birth were well within their domain.(31) In the "Sigdrífumál" st. 9 we read:

> Biargrúnar scaltu kunna,   ef þú biarga vilt
> oc leysa kind frá konom;
> á lófa þér scal rísta   oc of liðo spenna
> oc biðia þá dísir duga.

(You ought to know help-runes if you want to help and to set free a child from women you ought to cut them on your palms and clasp around her limbs and ask the *dísir* to lend aid.)

The very name "Hjördís," which means "the divine female-being of the sword" appears tailor-made for this theme in the *Völsungasaga*. This also seems to indicate some of the mythological nature of this material. We shall return to the figure of Hjördís under the section dealing with Sigurðr's reception of the sword fragments, but here it is important to realize the essentially mythological and cultic significance of Hjördís as a protector and nurturer of the spiritual essence of the *Völsungaœtt*—in accordance with her *dís*-nature.(32) Thus, Hjördís keeps the sword and carries the seed of Sigmundr until the boy is born into the safe environment of King Hjálprekr's (= "help-giver's") court.(33) The boy's physical entity is present, however, an all important ritual must take place before the boy may become truly Sigurðr Sigmundarson.

Rites of Birth

In the *Völsungasaga* we find the following statement concerning the events immediately following the birth of Hjördís' son: "*Konungrinn (Hjálprekr) varð glaðr við, er hann sá þau in hvössu augu, er hann bar í höfði ok sagði hann øngum mundu líkan verða eða samjafnan, ok var hann vatni ausinn með Sigurðar nafni*" (The king was pleased with it, when he saw the sharp eyes which he bore in his head and he said none would be like him or his equal, and he was sprinkled with water and given the name of Sigurðr) [*VS*, 13]. Besides the fact of Sigurðr's "sharp eyes," which is often a trait ascribed to great heroes in Old Norse literature,(34) we are principally interested in the formula: "... var hann vatni ausinn með Sigurðar nafni." Examples of this ritual formula, as it is found in the literature, have already been discussed in Chapter VII.

The actual method by which this rite was carried out is not explicitly stated in the texts, however, we may suppose that the new-born child was first laid in the lap of the father, or the chieftain of the clan(35) and then the child would be sprinkled with water and the name would be given, all accompanied by a ritual formulaic speech.(36) The word *ausa* seems to indicate that perhaps a ladle was used to pour the water over the child,(37) while the term *verpa* seems to denote a "sprinkling" action, but neither indicate the "dipping" type of rite used by the Christians.(38) It is possible that this rite took place on the ninth or tenth day after birth.(39) In the most archaic period the actual birth was also carried out in a ritual fashion, in which the child had to be born onto the bare earth (cf. ON expression: *liggja á gólfi*: "to lie on the floor," i.e., "to be in the cradle"), while the mother grasped the ancestral tree (cf. ON *barnstokkr*). The child would then be handed immediately to the father.(40) Here, we must only consider the twofold rite of birth and its significance for the *aftrburðr* ideology.

The idea that the child is laid in the lap of the father or chieftain, or that it is in any case a male who performs the actual rite of *vatni ausa ok nafn gefa*, is of great importance. The mother has brought forth the physical body of the child, and once it has shown itself to be healthy and worthy of legal status in the clan,(41) it is brought to the father, in order that it may receive its full legal rights (of inheritance, etc.) as a legitimate member of the clan. Until this rite was completed the child was only worth a portion of the wergeld ascribed to a "full-born" person.(42) Also the parents of a child maintained the legal right to kill the child (usually by exposure) if it seemed in any way less than normal,(43) The father then bestows legal "humanity" upon the child, and thus completes the act of complete birth, first by the acceptance of the child upon his knee and then by the subsequent rite of *vatni ausa ok nafn gefa*. The interval of nine days (if this is observed) is quite clearly a ritual representation of the nine months of the gestation period, however, from either this, or some other source, the number nine has generally come to be the most sacred and mysterious of numbers in Germanic religion and mythology.(44)

Now, the use of water in connection with this rite is of great importance. Water is probably the most potent single symbol for organic life and fertility.(45) Psychologically its relation with the concept of the anima and unconscious should not be overlooked.(46) Cosmologically, water, with fire, is one of the primal elements from which the world was formed.(47) Also, the three Nornir are said to pour water from the Urðarbrunnr over the World-Ash, continuously renewing it so that it will not wither and die.(48) It is interesting to note that here the term *ausa* is used in this context for "to pour." Moreover, we are doubtlessly dealing with a renewal process in which water plays a principal role. The connection of the Nornir with certain birth rituals involving the destiny of a newborn child have already been pointed out in Chapter V. The narrative concerning Nerthus in *Germania* ch. 40 is also indicative of water = renewal aspect. This passage also points to the close relationship between life and death with respect to water. Germanic mythology knows of the souls of the dead crossing water in order to enter Hel—also known as Niflhel ("Mist-Hel").(49) We are also reminded of the mythical ship, Naglfar,(50) and the practice of ship-burials and cremations in this context. From this evidence it seems fairly safe to conclude that the water is a potent symbol for life and the life energy which is active in the world of the living and dormant in the realm of the dead. However, it seems that this periodic respite is necessary in order that life may "revivify" itself. Thus, when the newborn child is sprinkled with water, it ritually comes into contact with the continuous life force present in the cosmic waters of Niflheimr. The child is renewed and revivified by its reintegration into the active aspect of this dynamic force.(51)

At the same time that the water is sprinkled over the child, a name is pronounced over him. This naming is also a reintegrative process, however, in contrast to the *vatni ausa*, which involves a more general "life-force," the *nafn gefa* is very specifically intended to reintegrate the child into the *hamingja* of the clan, and into the *hamingja* of the ancestor after whom the child is named. From a magical point of view the name contains the essence of the *hamingja* and when it is ritually spoken over the child it is done with the intention that the child should assume the qualities inherent in the name. Various aspects of the connection between the naming rite and rebirth have already been discussed in Chapters V and VI above.(52)

Although the entire rite consists of three parts (presentation to father, *vatni ausa*, and naming), these must not be analyzed as separate rites, but rather as phases of one continuous ritual of reintegration.(53) The presentation to the father is a dynamistic, sympathetic, direct, positive rite of integration into the legitimate social and legal rites and obligations of the clan. The *vatni ausa* is clearly a dynamistic, sympathetic, direct, positive rite of integration into the cosmic life force. While the *nafn gefa* presents a problem in the first category of analysis because although the *hamingja-fylgja* must have originally been conceived of as a dynamistic force(54) (as techniques of manipulating it usually show), in later times it was increasingly personified. Therefore, this phase of the rite would have to be analyzed as a dynamistic (with secondary animistic features), contagious (since the name-*hamingja* is manipulated and transferred as a concrete "substance"), direct, positive rite of integration into the *hamingja* of the clan, or of the ancestor after whom the child is named.

As far as Sigurðr is concerned, he is presented to Hjálprekr, a substitute father, who offers him protection by accepting him into the clanic structure under the king. However, Sigurðr retains his legal and spiritual heritage as a Völsung. It must be assumed that Hjálprekr performs the *vatni ausa ok nafn gefa*, although this passage in the

Völsungasaga (as is usually the case elsewhere) is a passive construction. The new-born hero has already manifested his integration with the qualities of his god-descended clan by his "*hvössu augu.*" Hjálprekr, by his ritual performances first integrates Sigurðr into the undifferentiated life force and then functions as an agent (as his name, "help-giver," might indicate) to reintegrate the young hero into the *hamingja-fylgja* of the *Völsungaætt*, by means of the name which he bestows.(55) Although Sigurðr is to some degree integrated into the *Völsungaætt* by this rite, he is still bound by laws of obligation concerning the avenging of his father. Before this vengeance (ON *hefnd*) is carried out the integration with the *hamingja* of the clan could not be considered complete.(56) With this particular rite it is unclear to what degree the ritual is an actual magical transference of power and to what degree it is a confirmation of the natural transfer of that power. It seems most probable that these two functions were understood simultaneously.

At this point, for the sake of continuity, we must turn our attention to three stages of the Sigurðr-material not directly concerned with the *aftrburðr* theme, but which are of some importance in the process of Sigurðr's integration into the *Völsungaætt*, in his manifestation of his Óðinic nature, and in his preparation for his most heroic acts—the slaying of Fáfnir and the awakening of Sigrdrífa.

Fosterage to Reginn

Sigurðr is fostered to the dwarf-smith Reginn in order that he might be educated by this wise, but non-human being.(57) Youths were usually fostered out to persons who had wisdom or craft to teach and the opportunity to teach it. The fact that Sigurðr is fostered to a dwarf-smith is of some importance since the hero comes into contact with a kind of figure often associated with the realm of the dead.(58) As a smith, Reginn may be considered an agent of renewal and initiation.(59) In various cultures the smith is a master of initiation—a shaper of young people and a type of advisor who is a reflection of the primal advisor.(60) One of the most interesting aspects of this fosterage involves the true nature and identity of Reginn. The Germanic dwarves are no mere elemental entities, they are complex and differentiated as to nature and function.(61) Also the god Óðinn bears a close relationship to the dwarves, and in fact the name "Reginn" is considered a *heiti* for Óðinn.(62) Reginn does portray many Óðinic features, such as knowledge of various arcane arts, and his urging of Sigurðr to kill his own brother, Fáfnir, etc. Although Reginn seems to be very Óðinic, it is not necessary to call him a hypostasis of the god. In any event it is important to notice that Sigurðr is fostered to a non-human being, who is a smith (perhaps an initiatory-renewal figure), and one who possesses occult knowledge, which he imparts to his ward.

Education

Sigurðr's young life is full of instruction in the field of numinous knowledge. In the *VS* ch. 13 we read of his learning *tafl*, runic lore, and the speaking of many languages. While in ch. 14 of the same saga we see where Reginn tells him of Andvari's hoard—thus educating him concerning the gods as well as laying the foundations for his future. Also in the "Reginsmál" sts. 20-25 we read the stanzas of wisdom and war tactics which Hnikarr (Óðinn) speaks to the hero.

All of these form important parts of Sigurðr's overall education toward becoming an ideal Germanic hero and king. The "Rígsþula" st. 41 mentions the importance of playing tables (ON *tafl*) as a kingly art, and st. 43 (among others) of that same lay attests to the necessity of runic knowledge for succession to Germanic kingship.(63) These teachings are probably of a more general type than that runic wisdom which Sigrdrífa is to impart to Sigurðr on Hindarfell, It is also possible that the languages (ON *tungur*) which Reginn taught Sigurðr were the languages of the various types of beings mentioned in the "Alvíssmál."(64) The tale of Andvari's hoard constitutes an important step in Sigurðr's heroic career in that it both gives him knowledge of an aspect of "world history" and informs him concerning his future task of slaying Fáfnir in order to retrieve the gold. Sigurðr's other teacher during this early phase of his career is Óðinn himself under the *heiti*, Hnikarr. This is one of the warlike aspects of Óðinn, and one which emphasizes his function as an agitator toward battle.(65)

This education in numinous knowledge is relatively unimportant in the rebirth process, but it is of the highest importance to Sigurðr's future role as an ideal king and hero. If we understand all of these instructional episodes under the general heading of "acquisition of numinous knowledge," then it seems that J. Fleck's demonstration of the necessity of this knowledge criterion for succession to the Germanic kingship would best serve to explain the occurrence of these passages in the *Völsungasaga* and in the *Elder Edda*.

Acquisition of Grani

The horse fulfills several functions in the religious symbolism of the Indo-European peoples,(66) and the horse sacrifice is known all over the territories occupied by speakers of Indo-European dialects.(67) Moreover, Sigurðr's steed, Grani, seems to be an aspect of equine functionality which was most highly developed among the Germanic peoples, e.g., the *Geisterross*, or *Totenschimmel*.

In the phase of the Sigurðr-material in question here, only the actual acquisition of Grani is of central importance. We find this episode portrayed in the *VS* ch. 13.(68) Whether or not this is a reflection of a cultic practice for choosing a steed must remain obscure, however, the mythic importance to the story of Sigurðr itself seems quite clear. The process may be analyzed in three stages: 1) the meeting with the *skeggmaðr* (= Óðinn), 2) the choosing, which involves a water test, and 3) Óðinn's revelation and prophecy concerning the origin and destiny of Grani. The words spoken by Óðinn make speculation concerning the nature and function of Grani unnecessary: "*Þessi hestr er kominn frá Sleipni, ok skal hann vandliga upp fæða, þvíat hann verðr hverum hesti betri*" (This horse is descended from Sleipnir, and he must be brought up carefully, because he will become better than every [other] horse) [*VS* ch. 13].

We may safely determine that the function of Grani should be analogous to that of Sleipnir. The Eddas portray Sleipnir as the means by which Óðinn, or his agents, are able to transverse the various worlds (or levels of being).(69) This seems quite similar to the function of the horse in shamanistic ritual, whereby the shaman travels to the "Realm of Shadows" on a hobby horse in order to find the soul of a dead, or sick person.(70) It is also noteworthy that an etymology for the word "Yggdrasill" (the name of the World-Ash, in which all the nine worlds are situated) is "the steed of Ygg (= Óðinn)."(71) This would further indicate the close connection between the horse and the idea of journeys to "other-worlds." In a socio-cultic context this is also indicated by the many horse sacrifices which accompanied the dead into their graves, or funeral pyres.(72) Also the use of horses in divinatory practices show their close relationship with the occult "other-worlds."(73) Grani is tested for his fear of water in the *VS* ch. 13, and later in the *VS* ch. 20 and 27 he will be tested for his fear of fire. Those two elements (water → ice : fire) dominate the cosmology of Germanic mythology as Niflheimr and Muspellsheimr, and through these two tests Grani demonstrates that he is indeed a being, in the mold of Sleipnir, which can transverse the extremes of the cosmos.

It must be emphasized that the acquisition of Grani is not a central event in the process of *aftrburðr* which Sigurðr is undergoing, but rather it is another in a series of Óðinic contacts which develop him into an ideal hero. The particular functions of Grani come later in the Sigurðr-material in the gold-taking episode (*VS* ch. 19) and in the penetration of the wall of flame in order to gain access to Sigrdrífa/Brynhildr (*VS* chs. 20 and 27). However, Grani probably should be understood as an integral part of the complex archetype of Sigurðr as an essentially "spiritual" or *hamingja*-like quality.(74)

Forging of Gramr

The *Völsungasaga* ch. 15 provides us with the principal text for the re-forging of Sigmundr's sword for his son. The "Reginsmál" (prose after st. 14) and the *ESS* (*Skáldskaparmál*) ch. 48 also include depictions of this episode, but they add no major new motifs to the theme. The Faeroese "Regin smiður" provides some variants, but it too follows the same general pattern.(75)

The *Völsungasaga* version describes what is essentially a threefold process: 1) the reception of the fragments from Hjördís, 2) the re-forging of the blade by Reginn, and 3) the testing of the blade by Sigurðr. When the young hero goes to his mother to request the two pieces of his father's sword, "*hon fagnar honum vel; talast nu við ok drekka*" (she receives him well, [and] they now speak with one another and drink) [*VS* ch. 15]. This seems to be a reflection of formulaic action which could be of more than incidental importance. Also after Sigurðr has formally requested the fragments, and just before Hjördís delivers them, it is indirectly reported that "*Hon kvað hann likligan til fama*" (She [Hjördís] said he was inclined toward fame) [*VS* ch. 15]. This too would seem to be a reflection of some *álög* or *atkvæði* which Hjördís spoke concerning the sword and Sigurðr's future deeds with it.(76) Once Reginn has completed the reforging of the blade, and it is brought out of the forge, it appeared as if " ... *eldar brynni ór eggjunum*" (...fires were burning from the edges). Besides the representation of the red-hot steel, this may also indicate the special "other-worldly" character of the sword. Sigurðr then submits the blade to two tests, which are almost universally represented in the literature—the splitting of Reginn's anvil (probably made of stone)(77) and the cutting of a clump of wool against a running stream.

Hjördís has preserved the slumbering *hamingja-fylgja* attached to the fragments of Gramr and at the proper time she releases the pieces, and the power, to her son. Examples of female figures preserving and handing down heirloom swords have already been noted in Ch. VII. In those cases where the mother in some way keeps the weapon for her son there is usually an *atkvæði* attached to the object—for good or evil.(78) The metaphysic for this custom is rooted in the belief that certain spiritual qualities are attached to these swords, and that not only the weapons, but also those spiritual qualities (*hamingjur* and/or *fylgjur*) may be inherited from generation to generation. The sagas are rich with examples of swords which seem to have a will of their own.(79) The sword also seems to function as a bridge between the worlds, or as a tool by which one's *hamingja* may travel. Here, we are reminded of the use of swords to dig into, and out of grave mounds.(80) The famous story of the Frankish King Guntram, which relates that, while the king sleeps, a small animal is seen to leave his mouth and go over a stream on a sword and into a hill, returning by the same path. The king awakens and tells of a treasure which is to be found in the hill.(81) In this instance the sword seems to be connected to a type of *hamrammr*-phenomenon. In the particular case of the Sigurðr myth, however, the sword is the primary symbol for the *hamingja-fylgja* which was originally given to the clan by Óðinn.

When Sigurðr receives the fragments he also takes on the same Óðinic responsibilities and destiny which his father took on when he originally grasped the hilt of the sword and drew it from *barnstokkr*. For, as we have already seen, the taking of a sword usually carries with it a body of obligations for the one who takes the sword—the *sverðtakari*. It is not suggested that we are dealing with a reflection of the *Hirðskra*-type *sverðtaka* ceremony in the Hjördís-Sigurðr passage, but rather this seems to be a continuation and/or inheritance of those obligations which were originally assumed in the Óðinn-Sigmundr episode. In any case, Sigurðr receives the potential power of his father's *hamingja-fylgja* from his mother in the form of the broken sword. Now, this potential energy must be converted into kinetic energy with the reunion of the two halves of the sword through the fire of the smith's forge.

Again, Sigurðr needs the aid of the dwarf-smith, Reginn. This is doubtless due to the special, magical abilities needed to re-forge this

117

other-worldly *Óðinsnautr*. Gramr, which was most assuredly originally forged for Óðinn by some unknown dwarf,(82) must again be re-forged by a dwarf-smith of equal skill. This situation may also portray a special constellation of interdependencies. In a Dumézilian sense it would show the dependency of the second function upon the third function in a craftsman role. Also the dependency of the human and divine orders upon the *dvergaætt*.(83) The other-worldly nature of this sword is perhaps emphasized by its name. "Gramr" essentially means the "angry one," but its etymology connects it with the concept of "thunder."(84) This may be an old remembrance of the cosmological importance of the mythic paradigm contained within the story of Sigurðr. In any event it is a good indicator of the nature of this other-worldly weapon.(85)

When the two halves of Gramr are reconnected, the *hamingja* which is attached to the sword again becomes active and rejoined to the Völsung-clan. This is more than literary symbolism, it is to be interpreted as a concrete reality which is totally consistent within the traditional northern Germanic tradition. In many ways this also constitutes a rebirth, because it is definitely a spiritual quality which is handed down from one generation to another.

The tests to which Sigurðr submits the blade of this weapon are also important. Essentially, he tests it against two extremes: against the hard and against the soft. This reminds us at once of the two extremes which also test the horse, Grani. In both cases we are dealing with an expression of the universal ("multiversal"?) potency of these entities, or symbols. Gramr is symbolically shown to be able to fulfill its function in two extremes of the cosmos. The two principal functions of Gramr in the story of Sigurðr are the slaying of the worm, and the awakening of the *valkyrja*—or more particularly the slitting of her byrnie which awakens her. Neither of these symbolically potent episodes fall within the scope of this work, however, their importance with regard to the two tests is apparent.

The reception of the sword fragments and the re-forging of those pieces into a whole, represent a composite rite of reintegration. Here, as elsewhere, it is impossible to be certain to what degree we are dealing with the reintegration or rebirth of various individual soul-conceptions and/or to what degree we are dealing with a gradual reintegration into an undifferentiated collective spiritual force. From the most objective point of view the latter would have to be the most probable conception.(86)

Prophecy of Grípir

The foretelling of Sigurðr's future by his maternal uncle occurs in both the *CR* (Gríp.) and the *VS* ch. 16.(87) There is of course a question as to the age of this material and the integrity of its inclusion in the Sigurðr-material, however, it must again be pointed out that the idea of a hero having his future foretold is a common tradition. In both texts Sigurðr goes and seeks out his *móðirbróðir* in order to receive his prophecy, and both texts emphasize the fact that Sigurðr had to force the prophecy out of a rather unwilling Grípir. This reminds us somewhat of the prophecies Cú Chulainn forces from Scathach in the *Tochmarc Emere* (The Wooing of Emer). The "Grípisspá" is presented as a dialogue between Sigurðr and Grípir in which the hero must entreat the wise one to speak each of his stanzas of prophecy.

This has little to do with the *aftrburðr* theme, but rather it seems to be another in the series of stages through which Sigurðr must pass in order to become the exemplary hero. The role and importance of prophecy has already been touched upon in the section dealing with Sigmundr's death above. Here again, it would seem that the prophecy of Grípir fulfills the magical function of foretelling and insuring the events of the future and it also functions as a indispensable body of numinous knowledge for the hero. The role of the *móðirbróðir* in this function of provider of numinous knowledge is well attested in the Germanic tradition. In the Háv. st. 140.1-3 we read where Óðinn is taught nine magical incantations by his maternal uncle. In this stanza it is emphasized that Óðinn learned these *fimbulljóð nío* from the son of Bölþorr who is the father of Bestla (Óðinn's mother).

Avenging of Sigmundr

The major texts which refer to the avenging of Sigmundr by his son, Sigurðr, are the "Reginsmál" prose after st. 25 and st. 26, *Völsungasaga* ch. 16, the *Nornagestsþáttr* ch. 6, and the "Regin smiður" sts. 100-103. In their major points, all these texts are in substantial agreement.(88)

As mentioned above, it seems that the *Vaterrache* episode finds many mythic parallels in the final stanzas of the "Völuspá," where the gods Víðarr and Váli take their vengeance upon the monstrous creatures which killed their father and brother respectively. Víðarr could be seen as the divine, exemplary model of the *Vaterrächer*, but besides this general comparison there also exist deeper correspondences. It could be interpreted that Óðinn "deposited his *hamingja*" in the giantess Gríðr in order to survive *ragnarök* and return to avenge himself,(89) just as Sigmundr may be seen as depositing himself (his *hamingja*) in Hjördís. The idea of a man or god avenging himself by this means is a powerful image. If it is true, as it has been suggested,(90) that Váli is the rebirth of his brother Baldr, then how much more would we expect this theme to occur in the father-son relationship? In any case, the myth of Víðarr expresses the necessity for vengeance in a cosmological context,(91) and at the same time makes the reward for the fulfillment of this obligation, *rebirth* (in the new-world in this case), clear. These mythological parallels further demonstrate the importance of the myth os Sigurðr as material for investigation into the religious traditions of the North.

The institution of vengeance must be further examined before a satisfactory interpretation may be ventured concerning this *Vaterrache* episode. Vengeance was considered a binding obligation for the surviving members of a murdered man's clan. Again we find that the avenger obtains special honor for his deed, and this may be translated into material, as well as spiritual rewards. In the *Svarfdœla saga* chs. 27 and 97 we read about two brothers who, after their father is murdered, decide that one of the brothers should avenge him and thereby inherit all the wealth of the father.(92) Vengeance is not to be understood as an essentially legalistic formula, but rather much more as a religious, or socio-cultic one, and one which is at the heart of the Germanic ethical "code of honor."(93) This honor, usually an unnamed but dominant force in the motivations of medieval Icelanders, can be considered a concrete spiritual force—which may be "stolen" and "recovered." It is taken away when a free-man in some way violates the honor of another free-man's clan. This honor may be recovered from the offender through an act of vengeance (or the payment of wergeld). However, it is important that the offender is capable of containing honor himself in order that it may be re-taken from him. For example, if a thrall killed a free-man, no true vengeance could be extracted from the thrall because he would be unable to possess any true honor.(94) The honor of all parties involved must be considered, however, the avenger would see his honor as just another part of the honor of the avenged. This honor is attached to a clan in much the same way the *hamingja* is attached to it. This is why when one part of the clanic honor is damaged, it is all affected, and why it requires obligatory vengeance.

120

Another aspect which may play a part in the vengeance concept is that of *aptrburðr*. When a man is avenged, and order is restored within the clanic structure, the *hamingja* and honor of that man is able to return to the clan. This is why, for example, when Þórðr avenges his father he is said "to grow great by the deed." The etymology of ON *hefna* "to avenge" may give us some clues in this regard. M. Sturtevant speculated that the word originally meant something like "to be lifted, or released from."(95) The idea of lifting or releasing certainly seems present, however, it is unclear as to exactly whom is lifted or released with reference to the semantic analysis of the word. Sturtevant says it is the avenger that is released (from further obligation), but it seems more in accord with the field of ideas surrounding this concept to say that the "releasing" is less specific and works for both the avenger and the avenged—just as the honor of both is considered in the motivation for revenge. It would seem possible that *hefna* describes a process whereby the honor and *hamingja* of the clan is restored to its proper order by retrieving the lost honor of the dead man—thus constituting a type of rebirth of this force in the clan.(96)

Aside from the vengeance theme, Sigurðr's battle with the sons of Hundingr also describes a heroic initiation, that of the first kill, or the first taking-of-arms. This was of course important in the Germanic world, and it was often the avenging of the father by the son which constituted this first act of warfare by which the youth justified his place of honor in the clan.(97) This institution was highly developed among the Irish where it was known as *cétgaisced* (OIr. "first exploit at arms").(98) The actual battle against the sons of Hundingr could then be interpreted as another rite of reintegration. The honor of Sigmundr is again reintegrated into the clan, and Sigurðr is integrated into the honor of his father, as a warrior.

Two other aspects of this section of the *Sigurðarsaga* remain to be discussed: the carving of the *blóðörn* by Sigurðr upon Lyngvi, and the feast following the hero's victory. The *blóðörn* reaffirms Sigurðr's connection with Óðinn since this was considered to be a mode of sacrificing the enemy to that god.(99) It is also important that Lyngvi is said to die bravely, with honor. The "Reginsmál" st. 26 (which is spoken by Reginn) reads:

Nú er blóðugr ǫrn   *bitrom hiǫrvi*
bana Sigmundar   *á baki ristinn;*
ǫngr er fremri,   *sá er fold ryði,*
hilmis arfi,   *oc Hugin gladdi.*

(Now the bloody eagle is   carved on the back(4)
of Sigmundr's killer   with a sharp sword (2);
no one is bolder,   he who reddened the earth,
with the chieftain's inheritance   and gladdened Huginn.)

The Nornagestsþáttr ch. 5 adds: "*Svá dó Lingvi með mikilli hreysti*" (So Liyngvi died with great valor). Lyngvi dies with honor and thus Sigmundr's avenging is complete and perfect. The feasts (ON *veizlur*) to which Sigurðr returns after this vengeance is completed serve as a fitting conclusion to this phase of his heroic career. The Germanic feasts were ritualized affairs in which formulaic speeches and songs celebrating the heroic past were performed. The function of this feasting (essentially consisting of the consumption of intoxicating drink) and ritualized speech seems to be the momentary focusing and realization of the confluence of past into present and present into past.(100) This could be interpreted as a point of reintegration for Sigurðr, in which the hero becomes fully and ceremonially assimilated with the *ættarfylgja* of the Völsungar, and the *hamingja-fylgja* complex of his father, as well as being reabsorbed by his society after his all-important *Vaterrache* and first-kill.

Footnotes to Chapter Eight

1. For a discussion of these three terms, see Ch. I.
2. This is a rather formulaic expression, however, it is established in earlier lines of the same chapter that the *blóð* / *sveiti* is indeed dangerous, when Sigurðr expresses concern over the *sveiti* touching him.
3. See W. Golther (1895), 567-568, on the practice of collecting the blood of a sacrificial animal in a vessel rather than using it directly for cultic practice.
4. Two of the most famous examples of this are found in Saxo and in the *Ragnars saga loðbrókar*. In Saxo (1931), Book II, p. 38, we read about Frotho who meets a "man of the country" who advises him to kill a certain dragon. The song the stranger sings to him reads in part:

> *Hic tenet eximium montis possessor acervum/ implicitus gyris serpens crebrisque reflexus/ orbibus et caudæ sinuosa volumina ducens/ multiplicesque agitans spiras virusque profundens./ Quem superare volens clipeo, quo convenit uti,/ taurinas intende cutes corpusque bovinis/ tergoribus tegito nec amaro nuda veneno/ membra patere sinas; sanies, quod conspuit, urit.* (Here, the occupant of the mountain guards an excellent heap [of treasure], a serpent, entwined in circles with numerous rings bending around and with a tail drawing out in winding whirls and shaking his many spirals and pouring forth venom [slimy liquid]. If you want to conquer him, then it is fitting, that you stretch the hides of bulls on your shield and protect your body with the skins of kine, nor should your limbs be exposed and bare to the harsh poison, his venom [diseased blood, cf. *sanguis*!] burns up whatever he spits upon.)

While in *Ragnars saga loðbrókar* ch. 3 we read about the hero's preparations for fighting with a serpent (ON *ormr*) in order to obtain its treasure. First he has a mantle and breeches made of fur and covered with pitch—and when he battles with the serpent we read: "*Þá kemr blóðbogi milli herða honum, ok þat sakr hann eigi, svá hlífa honum klæði þau sem hann lét gera*" (Then there comes a gush of blood between his shoulders, and that did not harm him because those clothes which he had made protected him).

5. J. de Vries (1961),567.
6. See *Bēowulf* 1606-1608. Also note that the word "*sveiti*' occurs as OE *swāt* in the meaning of "blood." This is a common definition for this word in the Gmc. dialects. In OHG we find *sweiz*: "sweat; blood.'
7. Cf. *Bēowulf* 897, with reference to Siegemund's fight with the *wyrm*, says that after the serpent had been slain it "*hāt gemealt*" (melted hot), presumably in its own "hot" blood. In *Bēowulf* 3041 we find a specific reference to a fire-dragon (*lāg-draca*) but this seems to be the result of foreign influence from the south. The typical Gmc. worm was a venom-spewing not fire-breathing creature. Cf. F. H. Whitman (1977), 276. Whitman speculates that the idea of corrosive blood was taken into Gmc. lore from Pliny, however, it seems that the monstrous, venom-spewing type of serpent and the identity between the venom, blood and sweat of

this creature is sufficient evidence to throw some doubt upon his hypothesis, and in turn postulate an indigenous Gmc. tradition of a venomous worm with corrosive blood.

8. On the magical properties of serpents' blood, see E. Ploss (1965) 35 ff. This is a common mythological motif. Cf. also Finn mac Cumaill's reception of second-sight through salmon blood in a similar situation, K. Meyer (1882), 201.

9. Cf. also similar passages in the *VS* ch. 19 and in the *ESS* (*Skáldskaparmál*) ch. 40.

10. See Ch. V for a discussion of the *hamingja-fylgja* complex and its role in the process of *aftrburðr*.

11. See Ch. V for further discussion of these factors.

12. See Ch. VII for a discussion of the motifs present in the *Þórðar s. hr.*

13. This is spoken by either Bragi or Sigmundr as they await the arrival of Eiríkr in Valhöll. Both Sigmundr and Sinfjötli are portrayed in Valhöll in this lay.

14. Óðinn's answer, i.e., the Fenris wolf will soon attack.

15. Cf. also the *Ynglinga saga* ch. 10 "... *gaf hann þá sumum sigr, en sumum bauð hann til sín; þótti hvárrtveggi kostr góðr*" (... he then gave victory to some, but he called some to himself [into Valhöll]; it seemed to each a good choice).

16. J. de Vries (1957), II, 58-59.

17. R. Auld (1976), 145 ff.

18. *VS* ch. 1. Rerir is impotent until he receives the apple which is sent from Óðinn by means of a *valkyrja* in the shape of a raven. It is significant to note that Rerir goes to a *haugr* (burial-mound) to receive this boon, thus the close relationship between tree, fruit, mound, and children is portrayed. Rerir then eats part of the apple and engenders Völsungr.

19. The name "Völsungr" is interpreted as "son of Völsi." Cf. G. Turville-Petre (1964),201. The name "Völsi" is a *heiti* shared by both Óðinn and Freyr, and it is obviously connected with their equine symbolism (*völsi*: "horse phallus') and their fertility aspects. Cf. F. Strom (1954), 64 ff.

20. For a discussion of this passage, see J. de Vries (1954), 95 ff. Also the parallels between this and the version of the Arthur-legend which appears in the prose *Merlin* (ca. 1450) are quite striking. In this tale, a great stone, upon which is set an anvil in which a sword is embedded, appears before a church. Upon this sword, in gold letters, there is an inscription which reads: "Who taketh this swerde out of this ston should be kynge by election of Iesu criste." Many lords of the land attempt to remove it, but to no avail. Later, the young Arthur comes upon the scene, unaware of the importance of the sword: "And as he come before the mynster ther the ston was, he saugh the swerde whiche he hadde never assaide. ... And as he come therby on horse bakke, he hente the swerde be the hiltes and drough it oute." Thus Arthur was elected to the kingship of Britain.

21. M. Eliade (1971), 17 ff., and (1963), 265 ff.

22. J. de Vries (1954), 104ff. It is also interesting to note a vegetative *heiti* which is used in connection with the sword, i.e. *ítrlaukr*.

23. This is the ritual by which a *þegn* (*sverðtakari*) swears his allegiance to his *herra*; cf. *Hirðskrá* and also H. R. Davidson (1958), 211 ff.

24. H. R. Davidson (1960), 9 ff.

25. H. R. Davidson (1960), 2-5. Here, several examples of the sword-tree complex in marriage ceremonial are provided. In one instance the husband thrusts a sword into the beam of the house—the depth of the thrust indicates the level of his potency.

26. W. Mannhardt (1963), 44 ff.

27. For an extensive study of this concept see F. Strom (1947). This study is rather weak in its analysis of the various soul conceptions which play a role in the power of the dying man, and tends to collapse all the various entities into one concept—*"hugr."*

28. J. Fleck (1971a), 119 ff., and (1971b), 385 ff.

29. H. R. Davidson (1960), 17-18, and Tacitus *Germania* ch. 18.

30. The *VS* ch. 11 provides an interesting example of both of these secondary functions in one citation. When Sigmundr is in his final battle it is said that his *spádísir* were protecting him—*spádís*: "a prophetic female divine being."

31. G. Turville-Petre (1964), 221 ff., F. Strom (1954), 32 ff., H. Hempel (1939), 245 ff.

32. It is not necessary to say that Hjördís is an actual *dís*, however, her role in the saga and her name combine to make it relatively clear that this is her intended function, and this meaning would probably not be lost to audiences of the 11th and 12th-centuries.

33. Hjördís was also able to survive, and find her way into good circumstances after the death of her husband, and thereby she assures protection to the boy.

34. This trait was also ascribed to Helgi (cf. HHI st. 6), Jarl (cf. Rþ. st. 34), also the description of Þórr's eyes in the "Þrymskviða" st. 27: *"þicci mér ór augom/ eldr of brenna"* (it seems to me that fire burns from [his ~ her] eyes). In *De Bello Gallico* (I.39.1) Caesar also mentions *acies oculorum* as a characteristic of Gmc. warriors (cf. *Germania* ch. 4).

35. This may also be reflected in the adoption formula known as *knésetja*: "to set on one's knees."

36. That is the naming itself with any other speeches, prophetic or otherwise, which may be reflected in the motif of wise women or nornir coming to a newborn child to speak its 'ate." (See *VS* ch. 8; HHI sts. 2-4; *Nþ.* ch. 1.)

37. There is a weak feminine noun, *ausa*: "ladle."

38. J. de Vries (1956), I, 137. The Gmc. word for "to dip" (Go. *daupjan*; OHG *toufen*) is usually used for the Christian rite of baptism at this time.

39. Evidence for and against the observation of an interval in the Gmc. rite with respect to its conventions in northern and southern Gmc. territory may be found in K. Müllenhoff (1881), 404 ff., K. Eckhardt (1937), 92 ff., and J. de Vries (1956), 1, 137.

40. J. de Vries (1956), I, 179.

41. The child demonstrates this through various signs of intelligence and good health during the nine-day interval. There seems to have been another practice, often confused with the *vatni ausa* which involved the dipping of a newborn baby in water—perhaps as a *"Härteprobe"*?

42. K. Eckhardt (1937), 87 ff.

43. This right was maintained in some Gmc. regions even after the coming of Christianity. Cf. M. Williams (1920), 57 ff., K. Eckhardt (1937), 81 ff.

44. Examples of the use of the number nine in Gmc. mythology and religion are many, however, in this context, the nine worlds of Yggdrasill (Vsp. 2; Vm. 43), the nine nights of Óðinn's initiatory rebirth (Háv. 138), Freyr's nine nights with Gerðr ("Skírnismál" 40), Heimdallr's nine mothers ("Hyndluljóð" 37), and the nine days of Sinfjötli's *hamrammr* initiation in wolf-shape with his father, Sigmundr (*VS* ch. 8), seem pertinent.

45. For a general discussion of water symbolism cf. M. Eliade (1963), 188 ff., and for a collection of diverse Gmc. lore concerning water and its mythological significance, see J. Grimm (1966), 583-601; 830-838.

46. E. Neumann (1963), 47-48.

47. *ESS* ch. 5.

48. *ESS* ch. 8, also Vsp. st. 19 in which *hvíta-aurr* is said to moisten, *ausinn*, the world-ash. This word *aurr* is used in both passages for the liquid which renews Yggdrasill. *Aurr* is probably derived from the strong verb *ausa*, however, it is also possible that *ausa* is derived from the strong masculine noun, *aurr*.

49. Often Óðinn himself is the ferry-man of the souls, cf. *VS* ch. 10. Also cf. H. R. Davidson (1943), 170 ff. for many other examples of river-crossing, etc., to enter the realm of the dead.

50. Cf. Vsp. 50 and *ESS* ch. 37.

51. Concerning the ambivalence of the passage from the realm of the "living" to that of the "dead" from a mythological or ontological point of view, cf. L. Gruber (1977), 330 ff.

52. See also Ch. VII for a general discussion of this rite in Gmc. literature.

53. The principles of ritual analysis follow those presented in A van Gennep (1908), 7 ff.

54. See Ch. V for a discussion of the dynamistic-animistic aspects of the *hamingja-fylgja* complex.

55. See Ch. V for a discussion of the thematic variance method of *Nachbenennung*.

56. See the discussion of the metaphysical aspects of *hefnd* in this chapter.

57. See Ch. III for textual references and a discussion of the *ætt* of Reginn.

58. H. R. Davidson (1958), 154 ff.

59. L. Motz (1973), 110 ff. Motz connects Óðinn with both the *dvergaætt* and temporally to the *Jól* festival of cosmic renewal; cf. also O. Höfler (1934). 54 ff.

60. M. Eliade (1962), 97 ff. The name "Reginn" has also been connected with the concept "to advise." See J. de Vries (1961), 436 ff.

61. L. Motz (1973), 100 ff.

62. H. Falk (1924), 24. Falk seems to consider Sigurðr's foster father an Óðinic figure.

63. See J. Fleck (1970), 39 ff. and (1971b), 49 ff., for a wealth of evidence demonstrating the knowledge criterion for succession to the Gmc. kingship.

64. These are the languages of the *Æsir*, *Vanir*, *dvergar*, *álfar*, and *menn*. Cf. also C. Watkins (1970), 1 ff.

65. H. Falk (1924).

66. J. Puhvel (1970), 159 ff.

67. W. Koppers (1936), 284 ff. Examples from Gmc., Indo-Iranian, Celtic, Roman, Greek and Slavic.

68. See Ch. III under "Regin smiður" for a variant of this tradition.

69. Cf. "Baldrs Draumar" sts. 3 ff and the *ESS* (*Gylfaginning* ch. 33 and the *Skáldskaparmál* ch. 25 .

70. M. Eliade (1972), 407 ff; 469.

71. J. de Vries (1961), 676.

72. For a general discussion of this, cf. W. Koppers (1936), 285.

73. For example the divinatory use of horses described in *Germania* ch. 10, cf. R. Much (1937), 135-38.

74. This is especially evidenced by Grani's close relationship with Sleipnir, the magico-cosmic steed of Óðinn.

75. See Ch. III.

76. See later in this ch. for examples of these *atkvæði*.

77. Larger anvils from this period were usually constructed from large stones. See E. M. Betz (1973), 174.

78. H. R. Davidson (1960), 5-9; and H. Falk (1914), 43.

79. J. de Vries (1956), I, 292 ff.

80. In the *VS* ch. 8 we read how Sigmundr and Sinfjötli dug their way out of a mound with Sigmundr's sword, and *Harðar saga* ch. 15 where Harðr makes his way into the *haugr* of Sóti by means of an apparently magical sword given to him by a certain Björn.

81. *Historia Langobardorum* III, 34.

82. Almost all swords in Gmc. mythic lore have their origin with the dwarves; cf. H. Falk (1914), 38 ff.

83. E. Ploss (1966).

84. J. de Vries (1961), 184. Cf. Old Slavonic *grùměti* and Lithuanian *gruméti*, both meaning "to thunder."

85. For a general discussion of the other-worldly weapon in Celtic and Gmc. tradition, cf. M. Puhvel (1972),210 ff.

86. V. Grönbech (1931), 1,127 ff. Grönbech consistently interprets the various entities and concepts within a larger category of *hamingja*. See Ch. V.

87. For a discussion of these texts see Ch. III.

88. See Ch. III for a discussion of the relationships of these texts.

89. The question of whether or not Víðarr is posthumous is answered somewhat by the special nature of the concept, *hamingja*.

90. J. de Vries (1955), 56. Cf. also E. Polomé (1970),63 ff. for a discussion of various aspects of the Baldr-mythos.

91. J. S. Martin (1974), 134; and G. Turville-Petre (1964), 64.

92. Cf. A. Heusler (1911), 51-52.

93. V. Grönbech (1931), I, 67-68.

94. V. Grönbech (1931), I, 69-70. Also the example given there from the *Hávarðar saga Ísfirðings* ch. 20, in which murderous thralls are let go rather than killed because nothing of substance could be gained from their deaths.

95. M. Sturtevant (1941), 262-263.

96. Here the "concrete conceptions" of both the *hamingja* and honor are apparent. Both of these entities may be released by an act of vengeance for a dead man, that they may again enter the clan.

97. V. Grönbech (1931), I, 119.

98. Cf. for example the *Macgnimartha Con Culainn* or the *Scéla Mucce Meic Datho*.

99. Cf. G. Turville-Petre (1964), 52.

100. P. Bauschatz (1976), 294. The interpretation of the Gmc. ritual feast presented in this article seems to lend itself quite easily to the idea that the ritualized activity serves to integrate men into a spiritual essence, much like the *hamingja*, which affects man, as well as being affected by him.

CHAPTER NINE

CONCLUSIONS AND PROSPECTS

Because this work is mainly intended as a study of literary artifacts, there have been several omissions of degree of emphasis. The archeological and anthropological evidence should indeed be further developed in order to give a more complete picture of the nature of the Germanic peoples' beliefs concerning the soul, and the rebirth of a portion of that soul within the clanic structure. Moreover, there are several other studies which are suggested by the present work, and which would further develop the ideas forwarded here. Also, there are perhaps further applications for the evidence and conclusions contained in the previous chapters in other works, principally works of Icelandic literature.

One of the studies which seems to be suggested concerns the Germanic concept of "fate" (ON *ørlög*, *förlög*, etc.) and specifically how it is perhaps connected to the Germanic soul conceptions outlined in Chapter V. More research could also be directed toward the *aftrburðr* theme throughout the entire *VS*, in order to trace how the divine *hamingja* of Óðinn found its way from Sigi to Sigurðr. The importance of the *valkyrja* Sigrdrífa/Brynhildr in this pan-*VS* survey is also worthy of deeper study. Also, the initiatory themes and their function throughout the *VS* seem to be key elements in the over all understanding of the metaphysics involved in the Icelandic version of the Sigurðr legend These institutions were briefly touched upon in this work, however, this was only within the limited scope of the Sigmundr-Sigurðr *aftrburðr*. A comprehensive study of all the initiatory themes and motifs found in the *Völsungasaga* would, I believe, reveal a more unified structure than was hitherto thought to exist.

The research found in the present work may also be further employed in several ways. It could provide a beginning for a search through other works of Icelandic literature, in which the *aftrburðr* theme is not overtly stated, but in which it would nevertheless seem to exist. The *Völsungasaga*, and other works which make up the Sigurðar myth had never before been cited as examples of *aftrburðr*, and there are probably dozens of other instances of this phenomenon concealed in the literature. The discovery of more examples might provide valuable keys for understanding the behavior and "fates" of many figures; and indeed the underlying structures of entire sagas might also become clearer. The genealogies usually provided at the beginning of the family sagas (and often omitted by popular translators!) would serve as valuable tools in this regard.

Of all the *fornaldarsögur*, the *Völsungasaga* seems to represent the clearest and most powerful statement of the heathen Nordic spirituality. It stands apart from the other sagas in its universal Germanic appeal, for indeed its roots come from all over the Germanic world and its branches extend back over all the territories occupied by the Germanic peoples. In the final heathen formulation of the hero Sigurðr Fáfnisbani, the Germanic prototype of the hero is complete He has, through accretion, or by whatever other processes, acquired all the necessary characteristics to be the wise, and warlike embodiment of an entire clan begotten by a god and destined to defend the world in its darkest hour . . . *ok hans nefn mun uppi, meðan veröld stendr.*

REFERENCES

Editions of the *IS* and *FAS* are generally those of Íslendinga-sagnaútgafan (cf. Jónsson, Guðni below). The edition of the *ÞS* is that of Unger (1853). In all cases passages from the sagas are cited by chapter number rather than page number in the editions used, so that any of the many editions may be used conveniently. The Neckel-Kuhn edition of the *Codex Regius* is used throughout except where otherwise indicated.

Anderson, Theodor M. "The Textual Evidence for an Oral Family Saga." *ANF*, 81 (1966), 1-23.

Askeberg, Fritz. *Norden och kontinenten i gammel tid Studier i forngermansk kulturhistoria.* Uppsala: Almquist &Wiksell, 1944.

Auld, Richard L. "The Psychological and Mythic Unity of the God Óðinn." *Numen*, 23:2 (1976), 145-60.

Barlau, Stephen B. "Germanic Kinship." Diss. University of Texas at Austin, 1975.

Bauschatz, Paul C. "Urth's Well." *Journal of Indo-European Studies* 3:1 (1975), 53-86.

——————————. "The Germanic Ritual Feast." In: *The Nordic Languages and Modern Linguistics 3*, Ed. John M. Weinstock. Austin: University of Texas Press, 1976, 289-94.

Best, R. I. and Osborn Bergin, eds. *Lebor na hUidre: Book of the Dun Cow.* Dublin: Hodges & Figgis, 1929.

Betz, Eva-Maria. *Wieland der Schmied: Materialen zur Wielandüberlieferung* (Erlanger Studien 2). Erlangen: Palm & Enke, 1973.

Birger, Norman. "Ynglingasagan: arkeologisk belysning." *Fornvännen*, 4 (1917), 226-61.

Birkeli, Emil. *Fedrekult i Norge: Et forsøk på en systematisk-deskriptiv fremstilling.* Oslo: Dybwad, 1938.

Boer, R. C. *Untersuchungen über den Ursprung und die Entwicklung der Nibelungensage.* Halle: Verlag der Buchhandlung des Waisenhauses, 1906.

Boor, Helmut de. "Die Handschriftenfrage der Þiðrekssaga." *ZDA*, 60 (1923),81-112.

——————————. "Hat Siegfried gelebt?" *BGDSL*, 63 (1939), 250-71.

——————————. *Das Nibelungenlied.* Wiesbaden: F. A. Brockhaus, 1972.

Buchholz, Peter. Vorzeitkunde: Mündliches Erzr̄hlen und Überliefern im mittelalterlichen Skandinavien nach dem Zeugnis von Fornaldarsaga und eddischer Dichtung. [Unpublished TS] Kiel,1977.

Bugge, Sophus. *Sœmundar Edda hins Fróða.* Christiana: P. T. Mallings Forlagsboghandel, 1867.

Caesar, Julius. *Commentarii De Bello Gallico.* Erklärt von Friedrich Kraner und W. Dittenberger. Berlin: Weidmannsche Verlagsbuchhandlung, 1961. 3 vols.

Campbell, Joseph. *The Hero with Thousand Faces* (Bollingen Series 17). Princeton: Princeton University Press, 1949.

Chadwick, H. Munro and N. Kershaw. *The Growth of Literature*. New York: MacMillan, 1940. 3 vols .

Chaney, William A. *The Cult of Kingship in Anglo-Saxon England*. Berkeley: University of California Press, 1970.

Cleasby, Richard and Gudbrand Vigfusson. *An Icelandic-English Dictionary*. Oxford: Oxford University Press, 1957.

Cross, Tom P. and Clark H. Slover. *Ancient Irish Tales*. New York: Henry Holt, 1936.

Crüger, A. *Der Ursprung des Nibelungen-Liedes*. Landsberg a. d. Warthe: Volger und Klein, 1841.

Davidson, Hilda R. (Ellis). *The Road to Hel*. Cambridge: University Press, 1943.

——————. "The Ring on the Sword." *Journal of Arms and Armour Society*, 2 (1958), 211 ff.

——————. "The Sword at the Wedding." Folklore,71 (1960),1-18.

Det Konelige Nordiske Oldskrift-selskab, ed. *Sturlunga saga: Efter membran Króksfjarðar bók*. Copenhagen & Christiana: Nordisk Forlag, 1906-11. 2 vols.

Dillon, Myles and Nora Chadwick. *Celtic Realms*. New York: New American Library, 1967.

Dumézil, Georges. *The Destiny of the Warrior*. Chicago: University of Chicago Press, 1970.

——————. *From Myth to Fiction*. Chicago: University of Chicago Press, 1973.

Eckhardt, Karl August. *Irdische Unsterblichkeit: Germanischer Glaube an die Wiederverkörperung in der Sippe*. Weimar: H. Bohlaus, 1937.

Einarsson, Stefán. *History of Icelandic Literature*. New York: The Johns Hopkins Press, 1957.

Eliade, Mircea. *Rites and Symbols of Initiation: The Mysteries of Birth and Rebirth*, tr. W. R. Trask. New York: Harper and Row, 1958.

——————. *The Forge and the Crucible*, tr. S. Corrin. Chicago: University of Chicago Press, 1962.

——————. *Patterns in Comparative Religion*, tr. R. Sheed. New York: World Publishing, 1963.

——————. *The Myth of the Eternal Return, or Cosmos and History*, tr. W. R. Trask (Bollingen Series 46) Princeton: Princeton University Press, 1971.

——————. *Shamanism: Arcahic Techniques of Ecstasy*, tr. W. R. Trask (Bollingen Series 76). Princeton: Princeton University Press, 1972 .

Ernst, Ludwig. "Über die Entstehung der mittelalterlichen Gedichte welche die deutsche Heldensage behandeln." Diss. Rostock, 1839.

Falk, Hjalmar. *Altnordische Waffenkunde*. (Videnskapsselskapets Skrifter II Hist.-Filos. Klasse No.6), Kristiana: Dybwad,1914.

——————. *Odensheite* (Videnskapsselskapets Skifter II Hist.-Filos. Kasse

No. 10), Kristiana: Dybwad, 1924.

——————. "Sjelen i Hedentroen." *MM* 1926, 169-74.

Finch, R. G. *The Saga of the Völsungs*. London: Nelson, 1965.

——————. "The Treatment of Poetic Sources by the Compiler of Vǫlsunga saga." *Saga-Book* 16:4 (1965), 315-53.

Flateyjarbók. Efter offentlig foranstaltning. Christiana: P. T. Malings, 1860.

Fleck, Jere. "Konr-Óttarr-Geiroðr: A Knowledge Criterion for Succession to the Germanic Sacred Kingship." *SS*, 42 (1970), 39-49.

——————. "Óðinn's Self-Sacrifice—A New Interpretation: I The Ritual Inversion." *SS*, 43:2 (1971a), 119-42.

——————. "Óðinn's Self-Sacrifice—A New Interpretation: II The Ritual Landscape." *SS*, 43:4 (1971b), 385-413.

——————. "The Knowledge-Criterion in the 'Grímnismál': The Case Against Shamanism." *ANF*, 86 (1971c), 49-65.

Flom, George T. "Alliteration and Variation in Old Germanic Name-Giving." *MLN*, 32 (1917), 7-17.

Gennep, Arnold van. *The Rites of Passage*, tr. M. B. Vizedom & G. L. Caffee. Chicago: University of Chicago Press, 1960.

Gering, Hugo, ed. *Eyrbyggja saga*. (Altnordische Saga-Bibliothek 6), Halle: Niemeyer, 1897.

Golther, Wolfgang. *Handbuch der germanischen Mythologie*. Leipzig: Verlag von S. Hirzel, 1895.

Grimm, Jacob. *Teutonic Mythology*, tr. S. Stallybrass. New York: Dover, 1966, 4 vols.

Grönbech, Vilhelm. *The Culture of the Teutons*. London: Oxford University Press, 1931.

Gruber, Loren C. "The Rites of Passage: 'Hávamál' Stanzas 1-5. 1 *SS*, 49:3 (1977), 330-40.

Gutenbrunner, Siegfried. "Altnordische Spruchdichtung in den 'Reginsmal.'" *ZDA*, 74 (1937), 135-39.

Halliday, W. R. *Greek Divination*. London: MacMillan, 1913.

Harris, Richard L. "A Study of 'Grípisspá'" *SS*, 43:4 (1971), 344-55.

Helm, Karl. "Altgermanische Religion," In: *Germanische Wiedererstehung*, Ed. Hermann Nollau. Heidelberg: Winter, 1926.

Hempel, Heinrich. "Die Handschrift Verhältnisse der *Þiðrekssaga*." *BGDSL*, 48 (1924), 417-47.

——————. "Matronenkult und germanischer Mutterglaube." *GRM*, 27 (1939), 245-70.

——————. "Sigurds Ausritt zur Vaterrache." *FestNeckel*, (1938), 155-69.

——————. "Sächsische Nibelungendichtung und Sächsischer Ursprung der Thidrikssaga." *Fest Genzmer*, (1952), 138-56.

Hendricks, R. A. *Classical Gods and Heroes*. New York: Fredrick Ungar, 1972 .

Hermann, Paul. *Nordische Mythologie*. Leipzig: Verlag von Wilhelm Engelmann, 1903.

133

Heusler, Andreas. *Das Strafrecht der Islandersagas*. Leipzig: Duncker & Humbolt, 1911

——————. "Altnordische Dichtung und Prosa von Jung Sigurd." Berlin (Sitzungsberichte 1919, 162-95).

, ——————. *Die altgermanische Dichtung*. Berlin-Neuabelsberg: Akedemische Verlagsgesellschaft Athenaion, 1923.

Höfler, Otto. *Kultische Geheimbünde der Germanen*. Frankfurt am Main: Verlag Moritz Disterweg, 1934. Vol. 1. [Vol. 2 never appeared.].

——————. *Germanisches Sakralkönigtum. I Der Runenstein von Rök und die germanische Individualweihe*. Tübingen: Niemeyer, 1952.

——————. *Siegfried, Arminius und die Symbolik*. Heidelberg: Winter, 1961.

——————. "Abstammungstraditionen." *RGA* 1:1 (1973), 18-29.

Hollander, Lee M. "Notes on the *Nornagestsþáttr*." *SS*, 3 (1916), 105-11.

Holmberg, Uno. Finno-Ugric and Siberian Mythology. In: *The Mythology of All Races*. Ed. J. A. MacCulloch. New York: Cooper Square Publishers, 1964.

Hull, Eleanor. *The Cuchulainn Saga in Irish Literature* (Grimm Library 8, 1898). New York: AMS Press, 1972.

Hultkranz, Åke. *Conceptions of the Soul among North American Indians: A Study in Religious Ethnology*. (The Ethnological Museum of Sweden, Stockholm Monograph Series 1) Stockholm, 1953.

Huss, R. "Die Senna der Königinnen in der Völsungasaga und in der Nibelungensage." *BGDSL*, 47 (1923), 506-07.

Jiriczek, O. L., ed. "Die Hvenische Chronik." *AG*, 3:2, 1892.

Johannesson, Alexander. *Isländisches etymologisches Wörterbuch*. Bern: A. Francke, 1951-56.

Jones, Gwyn and Thomas Jones, trs. and eds. *The Mabinogion*. London: Dent and Sons, 1974.

Jónsson, Finnur, ed. *Den Norsk-Islandske Skjaldedigtning*. Copenhagen & Kristiana: Gyldendalske Boghandel & Norsk Forlag, 1908. 2 Vols.

Jónsson, Gúðni, ed. *Islendinga Sögur*. Reykjavík: Islendingasagnaútgafan, 1949. 13 Vols.

——————., ed. *Fornaldarsögur Norðurlanda*. Reykjavík: Íslendingasagna-útgafan, 1950. 4 Vols.

Jung, Carl G. *The Archetypes and the Collective Unconscious*. (Bollingen Series 20, vol. 9, pt. 1) tr. R. F. C. Hull. Princeton: Princeton University Press, 1959.

Kahle, Bernhard. "Altwestnordische Namenstudien." *Indogermanische Forschungen*, 14 (1903), 133-224.

——————. "Die altwestnordischen Beinamen bis etwa zum Jahre 1400." *ANF*, 22 (1910), 142-202; 226-260.

Kålund, Kristian. "Familielivet på Island i den forste sagaperiode (intil 1030)." *AaNO* (1870), 269-381.

Kaufmann, Friedrich. "Über den Schicksalsglauben der Germanen. " *ZDP*, 50 (1926), 361-408.

134

Keil, Max. *Altisländische Namenwahl*. (Palaestra 176) Leipzig: Mayer & Müller, 1931.

Kendrik, T. D. *The Druids: A Study in Kelitic Prehistory*. London: Frank Cass, 1966.

Kock, Ernst A., ed. Den Norsk-Islandska Skaldediktningen. Lund: C. W. K. Gleerups Forlag, 1946.

Koppers, W. "Pferdeopfer und Pferdekult bei den Indogermanen." *Wiener Beitrage zur Kulturgeschichte und Linguistik*, 4 (1936), 279-412.

Kuhn, Hans. "Das Edda Stück von Sigurds Jugend." *Miscellanea Academica Berolinensia*, 2:1 (1950), 33-46.

—————. "Brunhild und das Kriemhild-Lied." In: *Frühe Epik West-europas*. (Beihefte zur Zeitschrift für romanische Philologie 95), Tubingen: Niemeyer, 1953, 9-21.

Kummer, Bernhard. *Die Lieder des Codex Regius (Edda) und verwandte Denkmäler*. (Mythische Dichtung Erster Teil, Bd. I. "Die Schau der Scherin"), Gisela Lienau: Verlag der Forschungen unserer Zeit, 1961. Vol. 1.

Lachmann, Karl. "Kritik der Sage von den Nibelungen." *Rheinisches Museum*, 3 (1829), 435-64.

Larson, Gerald James, ed. *Myth in Indo-European Antiquity*. Berkeley: University of California Press, 1974.

Lintzel, Martin. *Der historische Kern der Sigfridsage*. Berlin: Verlag Emil Ebering, 1934.

Littleton, C. Scott. *The New Comparative Mythology: An Anthropological Assessment of the Theories of Georges Dumézil*. Berkeley: University of California Press, 1973.

Lukman, Niels. "Ragnar loðbrok, Sigfrid, and the Saints of Flanders." *MScan*. 9 (1976), 7-50.

Mannhardt, Wilhelm. *Wald- und Feldkulte*. Darmstadt: Wissenschaftliche Buchgesellschaft, 1963. 2 Vols.

Martin, John S. *Ragnarök: An Investigation into Old Norse Concepts of the Fate of the Gods*. (Melbourne Monographs in Germanic Studies 3) Assen: Van Gorcum, 1972.

Matras, Chr., ed. *Føroya Kvæði: corpus carmi num færoensium*. Copenhagen: Munkgaard, 1951. 4 Vols.

Maurer, Konrad von. *Die Bekehrung des norwegischen Stammes zum Christentum*. Munich: C. Kaiser, 1855-56. 2 Vols.

—————."Üeber die Wasserweihe des germanischen Heidenthumes." *Abhandlungen der philosophisch-philologischen Classe der königlich bayerischen Akadamie der Wissenschaften*, 15 (1881), 173-253.

Meyer, Elard Hugo. *Germanische Mythologie*. Berlin: Mayer & Muller, 1891.

—————. *Mythologie der Germanen*. Strassburg: Verlag von Karl J. Trubner, 1903.

Meyer, Kuno, ed. "Macgnimartha Find." *Revue Celtique*, 5(1882), 195-204.

Motz, Lotte. "New Thoughts on Dwarf-Names in Old Icelandic." *Frühmast* 7 (1973), 100-117.

——————. "Withdrawal and Return: A Ritual Pattern in the *Grettis saga*." *ANF*, 88 (1973), 91-110.

——————. "The Craftsman in the Mound." *Folklore*, 88:1 (1977), 46-50.

Much, Rudolf. *Die Germania des Tacitus*. Heidelberg: Winter, 1937.

Müllenhoff, Karl. "Die alte Dichtung von den Nibelungen, I Von Siegfrieds Ahnen." *ZDA*, 23 (1879), 113-173.

——————. Rev. of Maurer (1881). *Anzeiger fur deutsches Altertum und deutsche Literatur*, 7 (1881), 404-09.

Munch, P. A. *Det Norske Folks Historie*. Christiana: Christian Tonsbergs Forlag, 1858. 4 Vols.

Mundal, Else. fylgjemotiva i Norrøn Literatur. Oslo: Universitetsforlaget, 1974.

Naumann, Hans. "Altnordische Namenstudien." *AG*, Neue Reihe Heft 1, 1912.

Neckel, Gustav. *Altgermanische Kultur*. Leipzig: Quelle & Meyer, 1925.

——————. *Vom Germanentum*. Eds. W. Heydenreich & H. M. Neckel. Leipzig: O. Harrassowitz, 1944.

Neckel, Gustav and Hans Kuhn., eds. *Edda, die Lieder der Codex Regius nebst verwandten Denkmälern*. Heidelberg: Winter, 1962.

Neumann, Eduard. *Das Schicksal in der Edda I Der Schicksalsbegriff in der Edda*. (Beitrage zur deutschen Philologie 7) Giessen: Wilhelm Schmitz, 1955.

Neumann, Erich. *The Origins and History of Consciousness*, tr. R. F. C. Hull. New York: Pantheon Books, 1954.

——————. *The Great Mother*, tr. R. Manheim. (Bollingen Series 47), Princeton: Princeton University Press, 1963.

Niedner, F. *Islands Kultur zur Vikingerzeit*. (Thule, Einleitungsband), Jena: E. Diederichs, 1913.

Olrik, Axel. *Nordisches Geistesleben*. Heidelberg: Winter, 1908.

Otto, Rudolf. *Das Heilige*. Gotha: Leopold Klotz Verlag, 1927.

Panzer, Friedrich. *Das Nibelungenlied: Entstehung und Gestalt*. Stuttgart: W. Kohlhammer, 1955.

Ploss, Emil. *Siegfried-Sigurd, der Drachenkämpfer*. Cologne: Böhlau Verlag, 1966.

Polomé, Edgar C., ed. *Old Norse Literature and Mythology: A Symposium*. Austin: University of Texas Press, 1969.

——————. "Some Comments on 'Völuspá' Stanzas 17-18. In: *Old Norse Literature and Mythology: A Symposium*, Ed. E. C. Polomé. Austin: University of Texas Press, 1969, 265-90.

——————. "The Indo-European Component in Germanic Religion." In: *Myth and Law Among the Indo-Europeans: Studies in Indo-European Comparative Mythology*, Ed. J. Puhvel. Berkeley: University of California Press, 1970, 55-82.

—————————. "Approaches to Germanic Mythology." In: *Myth in Indo-European Antiquity*, Ed. G. J. Larson. Berkeley: University of California Press, 1974, 51-65.

Puhvel, Jaan, ed. *Myth and Law Among the Indo-Europeans: Studies in Indo-European Comparative Mythology*, Berkeley: University of California Press, 1970.

—————————. *Indo-European Comparative Mythology*. Berkeley: University of California Press, 1970.

—————————. "Aspects of Equine Functionality." In: *Myth and Law Among the Indo-Europeans: Studies in Indo-European Comparative Mythology*, ed. J. Puhvel. Berkeley: University of California Press, 1970, 159-72.

Puhvel, Martin. "The Deicidal Otherworld Weapon in Celtic and Germanic Mythic Tradition." *Folklore*, 83:2 (1974),210-19.

Ranke, Kurt. "Ahnenglaube und Ahnenkult." *RGA*, 1:1 (1968),112; 1:2 (1968), 11 3-14 .

Rohde, Erwin. *Psyche: The Cult of Souls and Belief in Immortality Among the Greeks*, tr. W. B. Hillis. Freeport, New York: Books for Libraries Press, [1920].

Saussaye, P. D. Chantepie de la. *The Religion of the Teutons*. New York: Ginn, 1902.

Saxo Grammaticus. *Saxonis Gesta Danorum*. Haunice: Levin & Munksgaard, 1931 .

Schier, Kurt. *Sagaliteratur*. (Sammlung Metzler 78), Stuttgart: J. B. Metzler, 1970.

Schlauch, Margret. "The Rhetoric of Public Speeches in Old Scandinavia." *SS* 41 (1969),297-314.

Schneider, Hermann. *Germanische Heldensage*. Berlin: de Gruyter, 1934. 2 Vols.

—————————————, ed. *Germanische Altertumskunde*. Munich: C. H. Beck'sche Verlagsbuchhandlung, 1951.

—————————————., ed. *Edda, Skalden, Saga. (= Fest Genzmer)*, Heidelberg: Winter, 1952.

Schrader, O. *Reallexikon der indogermanischen Altertumskunde*. Strassburg: Trubner, 1901.

Schröder, Franz Rolf. *Nibelungenstudien*. (Rheinische Beiträge und Hülfsbucher 6), Leipzig: K. Schroeder, 1919, 1-58.

—————————————. "Mythos und Heldensage." *GRM*, 36 (1955), 1-21.

Schück, Henrik and Karl Warburg, eds. *Illustrerad Svensk Literatur-historia*. Stockholm: Raben & Sjdgren, 1933.

Schütte, Gudmund. "The Nibelungenlied and its Historical Basis." *JEGP*, 20 (1921), 291-327.

Seip, D. A. "Har Nordmenn skrevet opp Edda-Diktningen?" *MM* (1951), 3-33.

Smith-Dampier, E. M., tr. Sigurd the Dragon-Slayer. Oxford: Basil Blackwell, 1934.

Steiger, Karl. *Die verschiedenen Gestaltungen der Siegfriedsage in der germanischen Literatur*. Rothenburg: Hersfeld, 1873.

Storm, Gustav. "Vore Forfædres Tro paa Sjælevandring og deres Opkaldelses-system." *ANF*, 9 (n.s. 5) (1893), 199-222.

Storms, G. *Anglo-Saxon Magic*. The Hague: Martinus Nijhoff, 1948.

Ström, Folke. *Den Doendes Makt och Odin i Trädet*. Göteborg: Elanders, 1947.

——————. *Diser, Nornor, Valkyrjor; Fruktbarheitskult och Sakralt Kungadome i Norden*. Stockholm: I distribution almqvist &Wiksell, 1954.

Strömbäck, Dag. *Sejd*. Stockholm: Hugo Gebers Forlag, 1935.

——————. "The Concept of the Soul in Nordic Tradition." *Arv* 31 (1975), 5-22.

Sturtevant, A. M. "Semantic and Etymological Notes on Old Norse Words Pertaining to War." *SS*, 16 (1941),257-63.

Thorp, Mary. "The Archetype of the Nibelungen Legend." *JEGP*, 37 (1938), 7-17.

Tolkien, Christopher. *The Saga of King Heidrek the Wise*. London: Nelson, 1960.

Turville-Petre, E. O. G. *Origins of Icelandic Literature*. Oxford: Clarendon Press, 1953.

——————. "A Note on the Landdísir." In: *Early English and Old Norse Studies*, 1963, 196-201.

——————. *Myth and Religion of the North*. New York: Holt Rhinehart and Winston, 1964.

Tylor, Edward. *Primitive Culture*. London: J. Murray, 1913.

Unger, C. R., ed. *Saga Ðidriks af Bern*. Christiana: Feilberg & Landmarks Forlag, 1853.

Unwerth, Wolf von. *Untersuchungen uber Totenkult und Odinverehrung bei Nordgermanen und Lappen*. (GA 37), 1911

——————. "Namensgebung und Wiedergeburtsglaube bei Nord-germanen und Lappen." *FestHillebrandt* (1913), 179-87.

Vries, Jan de. *Studiën over Færösche Balladen*. Haarlem: H. D. Tjeenk Willink & Zoon, 1915.

——————. *Altgermanische Religionsgeschichte*. Grundriss der germanischen Philologie 12), Berlin: de Gruyter, 1937. 2 Vols.

——————. "Baum und Schwert in der Sage von Sigmundr." *ZDA* 85 (1954), 95-106.

——————. "Der Mythos von Baldrs Tod." *ANF* 70 (1955), 41-60.

——————. *Altgermanische Religionsgeschichte*. (Grundriss der germanischen Philologie 12), Berlin: de Gruyter, 1956-57. 2 Vols.

——————. *Altnordisches etymologisches Wörterbuch*. Leiden: E. J. Brill, 1961a.

——————. *Keltische Religion*. Stuttgart: W. Kohlhammer, 1961b.

——————. Heroic Song and Heroic Legend, tr. B. J. Tinmer. London: Oxford University Press, 1963.

——————. *Altnordische Literaturgeschichte*. (Grundriss der germanischen Philologie 15), Berlin: de Gruyter, 1964. 2 Vols.

Watkins, Calvert. "Language of Gods and Language of Men: Remarks on Some Indo-European Metalinguistic Traditions." In: *Myth and Law Among the Indo-Europeans*, ed. J. Puhvel. Berkeley: University of California Press, 1970, 1-17.

Weinstock, John M., ed. *The Nordic Languages and Modern Linguistics 2*: Proceedings of the Third International Conference of Nordic and General Linguistics, April 5-9, 1976. Austin: University of Texas Press, 1976.

Whitman, F. H. "Corrosive Blood in *Bēowulf.*" *Nph*, 61 (1977), 276.

Wieselgren, Per. *Quellenstudien zur Völsungasaga.* Tartu: Eesti Raamat, 1935.

Williams, Mary. *Social Scandinavia in the Viking Age.* New York: MacMillan, 1930.